Praise for *The New Reformation*

Shai Linne's *The New Reformation* is critical and encouraging, orthodox and challenging, empathetic and honest. Heartbreaking at points, humble and hopeful throughout, he even suggests what's gone wrong with so many who espoused the Bible's gospel and yet have missed it on race. I highly commend it.

MARK DEVER
Pastor, Capitol Hill Baptist Church
President, 9Marks.org

This book is classic Shai Linne. It is winsome and biblical, humble and theological, serious and sober. Shai graciously points out the sicknesses of a divided church and then encouragingly points to the only cure—an undivided gospel.

ANTHONY CARTER
Pastor, East Point Church (Atlanta, GA)
Author, *On Being Black and Reformed*

The New Reformation is a remarkable book that begins with Shai's own story and somehow manages to seamlessly integrate music, church, theology, Reformation history, current events, and personal experience into a compelling Jesus-centered narrative about ethnic unity. I found it engaging and insightful with wise practical advice. I highly recommend this book!

RANDY ALCORN
Author, founder of Eternal Perspective Ministries

What Shai has given us is a work that is theologically rich and yet incredibly clear. He begins with memoir, makes pit stops into history, ending with the hope of ethnic unity that transcends our current cultural divisions. The aim of his book speaks to Christ's heart for His church, making it a worthwhile resource for any and all Christians.

JACKIE HILL PERRY
Writer, Bible teacher, poet, and author of *Gay Girl, Good God* and *Jude: Contending for the Faith in Today's Culture*

Rarely, I read a book I wish every single person would read. Well, this is one of those books! I could not put it down. *The New Reformation* is a foundation of theological and practical wisdom. It accurately identifies the problem and it also provides a biblical way forward for all of us. I cannot commend this book highly enough.

DANIEL L. AKIN
President, Southeastern Baptist Theological Seminary

Honest, humble, helpful, hopeful, and above all rooted in a commitment to the authority of Scripture and a robustly scriptural discipleship of Christians in this area, this book sets out a beautiful picture of what the church can be. I was instructed, encouraged, motivated, and moved in reading it. I think you will be too.

LIGON DUNCAN
Chancellor, Reformed Theological Seminary

THE NEW REFORMATION

SHAI LINNE

FINDING HOPE in THE FIGHT for ETHNIC UNITY

MOODY PUBLISHERS

CHICAGO

© 2021 by
SHAI LINNE

Unless otherwise indicated, Scripture quotations are from the ESV® Bible (The Holy Bible, English Standard Version®), copyright © 2001 by Crossway, a publishing ministry of Good News Publishers. Used by permission. All rights reserved.

Scripture quotations marked CSB have been taken from the Christian Standard Bible®, Copyright © 2017 by Holman Bible Publishers. Used by permission. Christian Standard Bible® and CSB® are federally registered trademarks of Holman Bible Publishers.

Scripture quotations marked (NIV) are taken from the Holy Bible, New International Version®, NIV®. Copyright © 1973, 1978, 1984, 2011 by Biblica, Inc.™ Used by permission of Zondervan. All rights reserved worldwide. www.zondervan.com The "NIV" and "New International Version" are trademarks registered in the United States Patent and Trademark Office by Biblica, Inc.™

A version of the appendix was originally published on The Gospel Coalition website, June 8, 2020.

All emphasis in Scripture has been added.

Names and details of some stories have been changed to protect the privacy of individuals.

Edited by Amanda Cleary Eastep
Interior design: Erik M. Peterson
Cover design: Gabriel Reyes-Ordeix
Cover image: Timothy Wright

All websites and phone numbers listed herein are accurate at the time of publication but may change in the future or cease to exist. The listing of website references and resources does not imply publisher endorsement of the site's entire contents. Groups and organizations are listed for informational purposes, and listing does not imply publisher endorsement of their activities.

Library of Congress Cataloging-in-Publication Data

Names: Linne, Shai, author.
Title: The new reformation : finding hope in the fight for ethnic unity /
   Shai Linne.
Description: Chicago : Moody Publishers, [2021] | Includes bibliographical
   references. | Summary: "We all know that racial unity is important. But
   how can Christians of different ethnicities pursue unity in an
   environment that is full of landmines on all sides? In The New
   Reformation, Christian hip-hop artist Shai Linne shows how the gospel
   applies to ethnic unity"-- Provided by publisher.
Identifiers: LCCN 2020053399 (print) | LCCN 2020053400 (ebook) | ISBN
   9780802423207 (paperback) | ISBN 9780802499523 (ebook)
Subjects: LCSH: Ethnic relations--Religious aspects--Christianity. |
   Ethnicity--Religious aspects--Christianity. | Reconciliation--Religious
   aspects--Christianity.
Classification: LCC BT734.2 .L56 2021 (print) | LCC BT734.2 (ebook) | DDC
   270.089--dc23
LC record available at https://lccn.loc.gov/2020053399
LC ebook record available at https://lccn.loc.gov/2020053400

Originally delivered by fleets of horse-drawn wagons, the affordable paperbacks from D. L. Moody's publishing house resourced the church and served everyday people. Now, after more than 125 years of publishing and ministry, Moody Publishers' mission remains the same—even if our delivery systems have changed a bit. For more information on other books (and resources) created from a biblical perspective, go to www.moodypublishers.com or write to:

Moody Publishers
820 N. LaSalle Boulevard
Chicago, IL 60610

1 3 5 7 9 10 8 6 4 2

Printed in the United States of America

To Him who loves us and has freed us from our sins by His blood and made us a kingdom, priests to His God and Father, to Him be glory and dominion forever and ever. Amen.

Contents

Foreword

I love this book. Here's one reason why. I believe that our generation of American Christians will gain credibility to the degree that we come together in unity—a unity so surprising, so unselfish, so joyous it can compel the attention of our divided nation. This book calls us to that prophetic unity.

Our Lord prayed for us: *That they may become perfectly one, so that the world may know that you sent me* (John 17:23). Jesus will be honored as the One sent from the Father when we come together as one with a beauty our angry world cannot create. We have no right to settle for less.

But let's all admit the obvious. We often fall short of moving forward together as "perfectly one." We don't even know how to get there. That is why Shai Linne's *The New Reformation: Finding Hope in the Fight for Ethnic Unity* matters. This wise book helps us find our way toward the beauty that displays Jesus. It's a powerful missional strategy because beauty always turns heads.

Shai does not scold us. He wins our confidence, so that we dare to see ourselves and one another with new gospel eyes. Part of growing to fuller stature as individuals and as a generation is becoming more self-aware. In our youth, we naturally assume that our personal reality is the obvious reality for everyone. But as we grow, we discover how limited our own perceptions and intuitions can be. This aspect of adulthood does not invalidate our own ways. But it does humble us, as we recognize and respect other people and their ways.

In no way am I arguing for theological and moral relativism. All true Christians everywhere confess the Bible as the Word of God, the gospel as the good news of God, and Jesus Christ as the only Son of God. But even the apostles, as they grew in grace, understood more and more how limited their own Jewish culture was and how expansive the ministry of the gospel is. And as they matured, the gospel surged forward into the nations.

For example, in Acts chapter 2, Peter preached a Spirit-empowered sermon, with thousands of people converted. But in Acts chapter 10, at the conversion of Cornelius the Gentile, Peter saw the true reach of God's grace. He humbly admitted, "*God has shown me* that I should not call any person common or unclean" (Acts 10:28). And when reporting this breakthrough to other leaders in the early church, some of whom had their reservations, Peter defended his new sensitivity to human diversity very strongly: "Who was I that I could stand in *God's* way?" (Acts 11:17). And the other leaders "glorified God, saying, 'Then to the Gentiles also God has granted repentance that leads to life'" (Acts 11:18). Here is my point. The mighty blessing the church experienced in Acts 2 did not prove that they had a complete understanding of the gospel. It was later, in Acts 10–11, that their eyes were opened to how multiethnic the gospel really is.

In our own day, we are helped by these Scriptures to make full and joyful allowance for the entire body of Christ, with everyone being true to their own ethnicity and history and culture, and everyone rejoicing for Jesus' sake in everyone else, and all of us cherishing a unity together we never could have created on our own. And we are all humbled, careful not to absolutize our own backgrounds and preferences.

As we all stay true to the one gospel message while adapting to many cultural forms, our own limitations might prompt us at times not to divide but to free one another to take the gospel where each one can bear the most fruit—some of us in traditional settings, others of us in surprising contexts. But all of us can remain sincerely united in fellowship and support (Galatians 2:7–9). How glorious to be public cheer-leaders for faithful churches and Christians that are unlike ourselves!

This book is coming among us at just the right time to help us in just this way. Shai understands us and respects us in our differences. He doesn't shame us or pressure us to falsify ourselves. He leads us to Christ, according to the gospel, and helps us come together in ways long overdue. He pastors us toward rejoicing that God is gathering in so many people from so many human profiles. Then, in that place of unselfish joy, our unity is truly meaningful and clearly beautiful. And for me personally, if my own culture is reduced from prominence to mere presence, as one among many, I am not robbed. I can praise God all the more that, in the Body, so many ethnicities are given recognition and power for the greater glory of Christ.

As you read this wonderful book by my brother Shai, I ask you to consider this. If we Christians of this generation will be secure enough to honor our diversity, while also reaching across lines to show our unity, will we not be living proof that Jesus really is the Prince of Peace?

Thank you, Shai, for contributing to the next great awakening, which surely will be marked by a beautiful unity we have not yet dared to embrace!

RAY ORTLUND
Renewal Ministries
Nashville

Bumps in the Road

I wish this book wasn't necessary. As I write this, it has been more than a century since the abolition of slavery in America and a half century since the Civil Rights Movement captured the consciousness of our nation. Yet, the question of whether or how to address racial injustice in the United States still dominates our national conversation. We just lived through a summer that felt more like 1960 than 2020. We saw a Black man beg for his life and then slowly die with his neck pinned to the asphalt under the knee of a nonchalant White police officer. In response to this killing, we saw an unprecedented number of protests in cities around the world that went on for months. We saw rioting, looting, and destruction of property. We saw crowds of angry demonstrators clashing with police on the news. We saw protestors hit with rubber bullets, tear gas, and pepper spray. We saw the military deployed to urban areas and tanks ominously cruising up and down residential streets. While writing this book, on my way to work every day, I personally saw stores boarded up and soldiers in army fatigues with loaded machine guns patrolling the corners in my neighborhood. There was civil unrest not seen since the days of Rev. Dr. Martin Luther King Jr. Even those most optimistic about the racial progress we've made were forced to acknowledge that, after all these years, we still haven't solved America's race problem.

While I am grieved by what I see in our country, as a Christian with a biblical worldview, I am not confused by it. The Bible gives us categories to interpret and understand the world around us. On a basic level, what we are witnessing is the effects of sin in real time on a widespread level. This is what life has looked like since the fall of humanity in Genesis 3. If anything, I'm surprised that it's not worse than it is right now. Apart from multitudes of conversions to Christ and worldwide revival, I don't hold out much hope for anything beyond surface-level, short-lived changes regarding the sin that plagues our society. If our vision was limited to the chaos, hatred, and evil that we see in this world, despair would seem reasonable. That was certainly the conclusion that wise Solomon came to as he pondered life "under the sun." Solomon reasoned that it would be better not to have been born than to witness the evil so prevalent all around us (Eccl. 4:3).

City on a Hill?

Part of the church's role is to provide an alternative picture of what life looks like when a people are submitted to God's rule. Having entered the kingdom of God through faith in our crucified and risen Redeemer, the church has been ushered into a new existence, characterized by "righteousness and peace and joy in the Holy Spirit" (Rom. 14:17). This is the oasis that the watching world should experience when encountering the household of faith. But is this what they see? What answers are we providing to the questions they have concerning racism and injustice? And how does our lived experience with one another validate what we tell them? Has it not often been the case, both historically and presently, that the fault lines of ethnic division in the church and the world are indistinguishable?

Two Primary Concerns

In John 17:21–23, Jesus prayed for the church to be unified in order that the world might believe that the Father sent Him. This prayer request from our Lord informs the two primary concerns that prompted my writing this book: the unity of the church and the church's witness to the world. Because this is such a challenging topic, the temptation can be to shrug our shoulders with a deep sigh and give up, assuming the church will stay divided on this issue until Jesus returns. But Scripture doesn't give us that option:

"I appeal to you, brothers, by the name of our Lord Jesus Christ, that all of you agree, and that there be no divisions among you, but that you be united in the same mind and the same judgment" (1 Cor. 1:10).

Did you notice the command? ". . . that all of you agree." At first glance, that seems impossible. But in His grace, God gives us the power to perform what He commands of us (2 Peter 1:3). I firmly believe that all the tools necessary for the successful pursuit of ethnic unity in the church are found in the Bible. I hope to direct our attention toward those tools.

How to Read This Book

You should know up front that this book is written in a number of different formats. In earlier chapters, I share some of my personal story, which reads very much like a memoir. In later chapters, I delve into church history, theology, and biblical exposition. Another thing you'll notice is that when I speak of race and racism, I put them in quotation marks. This is not because I don't believe racism exists, but rather because those terms are loaded with unbiblical assumptions about anthropology. This may seem audacious, but I believe that a big step in addressing this issue is changing how we talk about it. Words matter. The terminology we choose can either be helpful or harmful to promoting understanding and effective communication. Over the years, I've found the terms "race" and "racism" to be a hindrance in this regard. I'm aware that "Black" and "White" as ethnic categories have their origins in the same faulty assumptions as "race." However, a full treatment of that discussion is beyond the scope of this book. Because of the way the book is formatted, I don't explicitly address these things until chapter 7, so I'm giving you a heads-up now.

Finally, while I stand firm in my convictions, I'm not writing as a scholar, and I don't consider myself to be an expert on this topic. I'm a fellow learner sharing some of my observations. I do believe that my experience in various ministry contexts, from church planting to pastoral ministry to Christian artistry, give me a perspective that I pray will serve the church of God. I believe in the priesthood of all believers. I write as a concerned Christian who loves the church to other concerned Christians who love the church. I also write from a hopeful perspective because I know how this story ends:

> *After this I looked, and behold, a great multitude that no one could number, from every nation, from all tribes and peoples and languages, standing before the throne and before the Lamb, clothed in white robes, with palm branches in their hands, and crying out with a loud voice, "Salvation belongs to our God who sits on the throne, and to the Lamb!"*
> (Rev. 7:9–10)

Having a clear view of our destination should inform the attitude we have as we travel there, even if the road is bumpy along the way. Once we get there, the bumpy roads will quickly fade into the rearview mirror. With that perspective in mind, let us press forward, eager to maintain the unity of the Spirit in the bond of peace.

Soli Deo Gloria,
Shai Linne

Part

MY
STORY
RY One

Chapter 1

Roses Are Big

"I have some news for you, kids. We're moving to the Northeast!"

My mother seemed genuinely excited about it. As she talked to us, my fourteen-year-old sister Shenita and nine-year-old me shared a knowing glance. Words weren't necessary. We immediately knew that everything was about to change, and we weren't happy about it. By "Northeast," my mom meant Northeast Philadelphia, which was literally on the other side of town, as we lived in Southwest Philly. In Philly in the 80's, the Northeast represented two things: The growing sprawl of suburbia fueled by the White people who had left the inner city a generation prior. And, for Black families like mine, it represented opportunity—the opportunity for better schools, better housing, better jobs. It also provided something of an escape for those who could see the writing on the wall as the early stages of the crack epidemic began to ravage our neighborhoods.

I definitely knew I was Black before we moved to Northeast Philly. But having brown skin didn't carry much significance in my preadolescent mind. It was just another fact of life, like wearing shell top Adidas, eating Apple Jacks cereal, or watching cartoons on Saturday afternoon. The kids in my neighborhood in Southwest Philly all had brown skin like mine. The magnet elementary school I attended (which was a thirty-minute train ride away) was extremely diverse. It was normal to see kids and teachers of many different shades, hair textures, eye colors, and accents. "Race" simply wasn't something we discussed. We were too busy learning the latest Michael Jackson song, practicing our "moonwalk," and looking for cardboard to breakdance on. But the Northeast was a different beast entirely.

When I walked into my 5th grade classroom for the first time that warm April afternoon, it was crystal clear that I was different. I could sense people staring at me. I could hear them chuckle. I was the only Black boy in the class, one of a small handful in the entire school. For the first time, being Black was no longer a simple fact of life like it was for Tootie in the 1980's sitcom. Instead, being Black was weaponized and used against me. Within weeks, as I was walking to the basketball court, I had my first experience (of many) of someone yelling "Nigger!" at me from a moving vehicle.

One of my earliest memories of my new school was walking into the lunchroom and seeing some kids huddled together and laughing. As I walked over to the group, a boy named Lance was reciting a poem:

"Roses are big, violets are . . ."

But as soon as Lance saw me, he stopped, his cheeks flushed with embarrassment. The group dispersed and I didn't think much of it. Later that day in recess, Billy, who clearly had less shame than Lance, came up to me, and, with a big smile on his face, shared the rest of the poem with me:

> *"Roses are big, violets are bigger*
> *You have lips like an African nigger!"*

All the other kids who were there exploded into uncontrollable laughter. I didn't cry in the moment, but the sense of belittlement and humiliation I felt still puts a knot in my chest more than three decades later.

Thankfully, incidents such as these don't represent the totality of my experiences in the Northeast. I developed good friendships with White and Jewish kids, and many of those lasted throughout high school, college, and into adulthood. For every Lance or Billy, there were a dozen Justins and Jills, close friends who treated me with the utmost respect and welcomed me like I was a part of their own family. And yet, as I grew from a ten-year-old into a teenager, there was a consistent, steady stream of experiences that would remind me that my skin color was viewed by many as some kind of threat.

Discipled by Hip-hop

I didn't grow up in a Christian home. My mother grew up going to church, but in her early adult years, she strayed from the God she had come to know in her youth. My sister Shenita and I were born out of wedlock. My mother held it down as a provider and did her best to raise us as she dealt with all the challenges that came along with being a single mom. But she hadn't imparted the knowledge of God to me, and very soon, other influences began to shape my eager young mind.

I grew up on hip-hop music in the '80s and '90s. I was especially drawn to East Coast artists who specialized in deep lyricism with a positive message. Artists like Eric B. and Rakim, KRS-One, and Public Enemy were in constant rotation for me as a youth. What I didn't realize as I listened was that not only was I enjoying their music, but I was also being indoctrinated in their often anti-Christian views. Unbeknownst to me, a form of discipleship was taking place. Now, over thirty years later, I can still recall the lyrics that were shaping my young mind.

I remember learning from Public Enemy that Farrakhan was a prophet. I remember learning from KRS-One that Black people in America wouldn't be Christians if their slave masters weren't Christians.

Before there was such a thing as "woke," being aware of the injustices that many Black people face in America was known as being "conscious." And I loved "conscious" hip-hop. It was lyrically dense, rich with soulful samples, and filled with explicit messages that aimed to inform the listener about the social ills of the day. Chuck D, the front man for Public Enemy, one of the more popular conscious artists, famously referred to their music and that of their conscious cohorts as "Black people's CNN." This stood in stark contrast to the so-called gangsta rap of the late '80s and early '90s that was popularized by artists like N.W.A. and Ice T. While gangsta rap emphasized and often glorified the vices that plagued the Black community (violence, drug-dealing, etc.), "conscious" hip-hop stressed a message of Black empowerment while speaking out against Black-on-Black crime. I connected deeply with this kind of hip-hop, which was neatly summed up in a phrase coined by KRS-One: "Edutainment."

By the time I graduated high school, my mom had come back to the Lord and began talking to me about coming to church. But at that point, my worldview was solidified; I was decidedly anti-Christian. Hip-hop had successfully catechized me. Hip-hop taught me that Islam was a better (and cooler) choice than Christianity. Hip-hop taught me that Christianity was the White man's religion. Hip-hop taught me that there were many roads to God. Hip-hop taught me that the Bible wasn't reliable. My attitude toward my mom was basically, "If that Christian stuff works for you, cool. But don't try to push it off on me." This attitude remained with me, and my hostility toward Christianity only increased during college.

College Life: "Spiritual" and Still Black

The University of the Arts in Philadelphia, where I studied theater, had two departments: the visual arts (painting, illustration, animation, graphic design, etc.) and the performing arts (theater, dance, vocal performance, musicianship, etc.). Although I was a theater major, I tended to spend more time with friends in the visual arts department. I've always had a pretty low-key, laid-back personality, so it shouldn't have been surprising that I found theater people a bit too dramatic for me. What I appreciated most about my visual artist friends was the kinds of in-depth conversations we would have. More often than not, our conversations usually gravitated toward something dealing with the intersection of "race," religion, and hip-hop. As I think about it now, these themes have formed a through line in my life, evident even in the fact that I'm writing this book.

By the time I got to college, I was pretty clear on where I stood on religion. First of all, I wasn't religious; I was "spiritual," thank you very much. And, I was agnostic. My favorite rapper, KRS-One, talked about metaphysics a lot. I didn't really know what metaphysics was (still don't), but it sounded like something deep to say when someone asked me what I believed. I had read *The Celestine Prophecy* by James Redfield and of course that made me a guru on all things New Age. I also read the Tao Te Ching and went on a Buddhist meditation retreat in the mountains of Santa Fe, New Mexico, not to mention making it almost halfway through *The Art of War* by Sun Tzu. So in my mind, I was also an expert on eastern philosophy. Finally, I was a vegetarian and had dreadlocks. Those two things *had* to increase my spiritual index. Basically, I had something of a salad bar theology. Pick and choose what works for me from all religions (except Christianity, of course) and throw it onto my spiritual plate.

In college, I was far removed from my "roses are big" days. The White college students I interacted with prided themselves on not having an iota of racism in their hearts. My Blackness wasn't weaponized against me at school. If anything, it went more in the opposite direction, toward fetishization. Yet, even while at college, I was reminded that Lances and Billys don't stay children. They grow up, often living lives with the "roses are big" mindsets fully intact and unchallenged by meaningful interactions with people of color.

One day, I was walking alone in broad daylight down a street in center city Philadelphia to visit some friends who lived in off-campus housing. I was coming from a rehearsal for a play I was working on. I had my headphones on. Since it was the mid-'90s, I must have been playing *The Score* by The Fugees, *Stakes Is High* by De La Soul, or *Illadelph Halflife* by The Roots. As I walked up the side street toward my friends' house, music blasting in my ears, I caught some movement just to the right. I looked over my shoulder and saw a police officer jogging up the street in my direction. My first thought was, "I wonder what happened up the block." Maybe I was lulled into some kind of detachment from reality by Lauryn Hill serenading my eardrums with "Killing Me Softly," but it never even occurred to me that he might be coming after me because, well, *I hadn't done anything.*

I was quickly snatched out of that fleeting moment of obliviousness. The officer grabbed me and yelled, "Up against the wall!" Within moments, what seemed like a fleet of police cars lined the tiny street my friends lived on. They were coming for *me*! Before I could even ask what was going on, my book bag was confiscated, and I was handcuffed and thrown into the back of a police cruiser. When I tried to ask questions, one of the officers said, "Shut up!" It would be many years later that I would educate myself about things like the Fourth Amendment and probable cause, but something tells me that having that information then would not have helped me.

It's funny what can go through your mind when your hands are cuffed behind your back in a cop car and you haven't been told why. I knew I hadn't done anything on *that* day. But that didn't make me completely innocent. I was in a party crowd and smoked weed regularly. But how could they know that? Had they been following me? Did they tap my phone? Was this about me writing graffiti in high school? Was this about . . . wait a second . . . my backpack! I had a prop gun from another play I was working on in my backpack! What were they going to think?

My speculation was brought to a halt when another unmarked car slowly pulled up beside the police cruiser I sat in. This time, a young White couple got out and approached the window next to where I sat. Suddenly it became clear. They were there to identify me as a suspect in some crime! When they got to the window, Officer Shut up! said, "Hey! Look over here." I turned my head to face the freshly traumatized couple. Surely, it was only a few seconds, but in those few moments, time stood still. How did I get here? Just moments earlier I had been reciting Shakespeare.

Now my fate was in the hands of two people who had just been victimized. All they had to say was, "Yes. That's him," and the entire course of my life might have changed in a moment. A felony charge. Expelled from school. Sitting in county jail until trial because my mom couldn't afford bail. The gut-wrenching choice of pleading guilty to something I didn't do to get less time or risking years in prison by taking it before a jury. A felony conviction following me like an obsessed stalker for the rest of my life, affecting future job, housing, income, and girlfriend prospects. All of these things were on the table, as far as I was concerned.

Also, given the shock of whatever just happened to them, would they be able to properly identify the person? Were they the type who think all Black people look alike? Was this robbery or assault (or whatever it was that caused ten police cars to pull up on me) the first time this couple had ever interacted with a young

Black male? I've never felt more vulnerable and helpless than in those few seconds. My emotions ran the gamut from fear to anger to sadness to disbelief to dread. I even felt empathy for the couple, as it was clear that someone had violated them. *But it wasn't me!* Our eyes locked. They looked at each other. Then back at me. And back at each other. Finally, as my life was flashing before me for the eighth time, the man turned to the cop and said, "No, that's not him." And with that, they stepped away from the window. A few minutes later, the sergeant pulled me out of the back seat. After he uncuffed me, he looked me in the eye and said something to me that crystallized not only this entire event, but all the "racism" I had ever experienced up to that point.[1]

After he uncuffed me, the sergeant looked me in the eye, and with a half smirk dismissively said, "See! That worked out well for you, didn't it?" No explanation as to why I was stopped, and certainly no apology. Just, "That worked out well for you." Well, no, sergeant, I thought. That actually did not work out well for me. I might, perhaps, think that it worked out well for me if I actually committed the crime and they failed to identify me. Or maybe if I was engaged in some other criminal activity at the time, I might think it worked out well for me. But as a person who had never been arrested before, let alone spent any time in jail; as a person who abhorred violence outside of Tarantino films; as a person who heeded my mom's advice when she repeatedly told me as a teenager, "Whatever you do, don't get caught up in the system, son. Once you get in, that stays with you forever and you never really get out"; as a person who was minding his own business and had just been scared to death by the police, no. I did not think it "worked out well" for me.

His question implied that my primary outlook as I walked away from this should be gratitude rather than what it actually was—trauma. His question did not (and I suppose, could not) take into account the person who was standing before him. Had he actually known me, I can't imagine him saying such a thing. All he knew was what I looked like and that I "fit the description" of so many others he had arrested previously.

After he said that, he handed me my backpack (prop gun and all . . . had they even checked the bag?), and I walked the final half block to my friends' house, where I had quite a story to tell them.

College Dropout

As I mentioned earlier, hip-hop discipled me in many ways. One of the other lessons I learned was that regularly smoking marijuana (or "blunts") came along with the culture. That practice, combined with the free-spirited lifestyles of my new artistic college friends, meant that every day of college was a party. This caught up with me when, in my junior year, with three semesters left until graduation, I basically partied my way out of school. I dropped one too many classes (an 8:30 a.m. class, completely unreasonable for someone who partied until 4 a.m. every day), which put me under the required credits for financial aid. And, just like that, my college career was over.

After I dropped out, I started a theater company with some friends and alumni from UArts. We put on a few productions, and we were beginning to make a bit of a name for ourselves in the Philly theater scene. However, I felt like things were moving too slowly, and I wanted to get out of Philly. So I came up with a plan.

I would move to Spain to pursue acting (and Spanish women). After seeing the world a little bit, I would return to New York and launch my career as an independent film actor and director. My youthful arrogance had me convinced that all this was absolutely going to happen. It was just a matter of time. So I started taking conversational Spanish classes and preparing for the move.

I was good friends with a guy named Carlos. We ran together in the same crowd at college. Around the same time I dropped out, Carlos had abruptly moved to a small city in the deep South, of all places. When I told him about my plans, he suggested I move to live with him. I could stay at his place, rent free, and save up money for Spain. That made sense to me, so I packed my stuff and headed south. This was quite the culture shock for me coming from Philly. Everything felt so slow. There was really nothing to do but get drunk and high. So, I found the party crowd there and that's what I did. Little did I know that God was sending me to the deep South to have an encounter with Jesus.

The Light of Christ Is a Blazin' One

Life in the South became routine very quickly. I got temp jobs in order to save money. I would work second shift from 3 to 11, get off work and head to our apartment, where there was a party every night. Get drunk and high, stay up until 5 a.m. or so, sleep until 1 or 2 p.m., go back to work and do it all over again the next day.

In our circle of friends, there was a girl named Heather. Heather was friends with Carlos's girlfriend at the time. She was also an outspoken Christian. This was the first time that I ever had an evangelistic Christian among my peers. I had other friends who got saved, but once that happened, they usually stopped hanging out with me. Most of the Christians I met were content to keep their beliefs to themselves. Not so with Heather. For her, it seemed like her Christianity was central to her identity. A few things struck me about Heather. She would always hang around us, but she wouldn't participate in our partying. She would come to the parties and rather than get drunk with us, she would drink a soda or a cup of water and just hang out. Heather was *joyful* and genuinely kind. Not kind in the sense that she wanted something from you and thought kindness was the way to get it. No, she was just a kind person, period.

She stood out in my crowd; we were usually sarcastic, cynical, and downright mean. To my shame, we did not treat her well. Everyone in my circle was in general agreement that Christianity was ridiculous, if not offensive. (What I later came to realize is that it wasn't "Christianity" I hated. It was Christ Himself.) A Christian in our circles was like a bloody fish in the midst of piranhas. We clowned her all the time, making fun of her, both behind her back and to her face. Heather's response to it was something I had never seen before. She returned all of our mockery and insults with nothing but kindness. I didn't understand it and it made me pause and ask myself, "What's up with this girl?"

One night we were at a party in Carlos's apartment. I was high on LSD. Before that night, if you would have asked me if I believed in good and evil, in my salad bar/pseudo-New Age worldview, I would have answered, "No. I don't believe there's such a thing as objective evil, or evil for its own sake. I believe that there are simply different levels of good." However, as I sat in Carlos's living room that night and looked around the room, I got the keen sense that I was in the presence of the demonic. This sense cut through all of my philosophical presuppositions and arrested me on the spot. I was terrified. I went out on the balcony to clear my mind. As I was out there, I began to think about some of the things my mom had told me years before.

I realized two things that night: *Trying to run my own life wasn't working.* The best Shai could do on his own was drop out of college, get drunk and high every day, and end up down South on a balcony with something demonic in the living room. And, *I had rejected the Bible without ever reading it for myself.* I had so many arguments against Christianity. In fact, I liked debating with Christians to try to make them look foolish. But all the arguments I had against the Bible were things that had been told to me by others (mostly KRS-One). I was just repeating their arguments. I had never actually picked up a Bible and read it! The foolishness of that hit me like a Dr. Dre snare drum. How could I reject something without even looking into what it teaches?

Not long after that night, I walked into a Borders bookstore and grabbed a Bible for the first time. I found a chair, sat down, and began to read. I had no idea where to begin, so I just opened to the middle (I don't recommend studying the Bible this way! But God met me where I was). The first thing that I remember reading is Psalm 25:7, where David prays, "Do not remember the sins of my youth or my acts of rebellion" (csb). This verse cut me to the heart. It became clear to me that I was rebellious and that I had rejected God my whole life. I snatched His blessings every day, and like the nine lepers in Luke 17, never once returned to give Him thanks. As I read, God was beginning to open up my eyes to who He is and who I am, in light of Him. Funny enough, as I was reading the Bible at Borders, Heather and a friend walked up to me. Heather had a huge smile on her face. She didn't say much, but I could tell she was really excited. I didn't get it at the time, but I do now. She had obviously been praying for her "party crowd" friends, and here was the one who was perhaps the most hostile to Christianity, sitting there reading the Bible.

I let my mom know what was going on, and she sent me a care package, including a small booklet that contained the gospel of John. This seemed easy enough, so I began to read it. In fact, I spent all my free time reading through John. Back at Carlos's apartment, there would be parties going on in the living room, and I would be in my bedroom reading through John. As I read, I was confronted with the person of Jesus Christ and His claims about Himself. I was mesmerized. Truly, no one ever spoke like this man! I was also confronted with how ignorant I was about what the Bible teaches. I was floored when I learned that Jesus is God, the Word who became flesh.

Everything about Him demonstrated that He was the embodiment of divinity. His wisdom and understanding; His authority; His power over nature; His ability to know people's thoughts; His prophecies; His humility and compassion. When I read of His sacrificial death and victorious resurrection, it was like truth being injected into my lifeless veins. It was self-authenticating in a way that caused me to believe and accept it as infallibly true. As I finished the book of John, I knew without question that I owed all my allegiance to this precious Jesus and that it would be my highest honor to be His follower. It was right there, in my bedroom, as I read of the person and work of Christ, that I was born again from above and transferred from the domain of darkness to the kingdom of light. This was March of 1999.

Within a few weeks, I was back in Philadelphia, a completely different person. I had been miraculously transformed. When I left to live with Carlos, I was a Jesus-hating, New Age–embracing, weed-smoking hedonist. When I returned, I was on fire for the Lord Jesus Christ and ready to tell everyone about Him. What I didn't realize at the time was that God, in His mercy (and with His sense of humor), was about to use the very thing that discipled me in my hatred for Him as the means through which I would help proclaim His supremacy: hip-hop.

Chapter 2

My New Life

Back in Philly...

Me: "Yo Harold! I got some news for you, man!"

Harold: "What's up?"

Me: "I got saved, man! I'm a Christian!"

Harold: "For real?"

Me: "Yeah, yo!"

Harold: "Praise God, man!"

Me: "And guess what? I'm back in Philly."

Harold: "You are?"

Me: "Yeah, let's link up so I can tell you everything. Matter fact, whatcha doing now?"

Harold: "I'm chillin."

Me: "Meet me downtown at the Clothes Pin in an hour."

Harold: "All right, bet. See you then. Peace."

Harold was one of my best friends from UArts. He was a visual artist I spent a lot of time around when we were in school. We would party together and often engage in "deep" conversations. Well, they seemed deep. We were usually smoking marijuana when we had them. I genuinely enjoyed being around him. But all that changed when he became a Christian during my junior year. He was the first in our circle to come to Christ. And this immediately drove a wedge between us. He stopped hanging around us as much. And while I was still cordial with him, I really didn't want anything to do with him anymore. In fact, when I would see him coming down the street or in the hallway at school, I would try to avoid him. I had no interest whatsoever in hearing anything about Jesus. By the time I left for the South, our close friendship had devolved into passing acquaintances. But once I came to know the Lord, Harold was one of the first people I sought out.

We met at the Clothes Pin, a huge statue and landmark right across from Philadelphia's city hall. As we walked to Starbucks, I began sharing my testimony and what the Lord had done for me when I was down South. I was seeing the world with new eyes, and all I wanted was to know more and more about Jesus. When I got back to Philly, I temporarily moved back in with my mom. I started going to her church, which was in many ways a traditional Black church with Baptist roots, though it had transitioned to being non-denominational. Harold and I rejoiced as I told him about how the Lord called me out of darkness into His marvelous light. One Sunday evening, Harold invited me to come to an evening service that he regularly attended.

Me: "What's the name of the church?"

Harold: "Tenth."

Me: "Tenth?"

Harold: "Yeah. Tenth Presbyterian."

Me: "Oh, okay."

I'm sure I must have had a puzzled look on my face. At that point, I didn't know the difference between a Presbyterian and a pescatarian.

Harold said, "You should come, man. It's dope. The people are a little stuffy, and it's kind of dry, but the teaching is dope."

As a new believer, I was so hungry for the Word that it didn't matter. "Let's do it!"

The first thing I noticed once I walked into the church was how *quiet* it was. My mom's church (Freedom Christian Bible Fellowship) was the only church experience I had in my few weeks as a new believer. There are many words I could use to describe Freedom, but quiet was definitely not one of them! The first Sunday after I got back to Philly, I was so excited that the Lord had saved me, I couldn't wait to go to church for the first time as a Christian. When I walked into Freedom, I was greeted with many smiles and warm hugs. It felt like they already knew me, because, well, they did. My mom had been praying for my salvation for over a decade. She had often requested prayer on my behalf from the brothers and sisters there.

Over the years, as I plunged deeper and deeper into sin, they carried her burdens many times. And, there I was, a brand-new Christian. One church mother, with tears in her eyes, embraced me. "We've been praying for you, young man. Glory to God!

Hallelujah!" As the service began, I looked around, amazed. I saw newly discovered brothers and sisters in Christ celebrating the Lord who saved them. There was singing, dancing, and shouting. The songs were all new to me, but as soon as I caught the melody, I joined right in.

As I sang, I was so overcome with emotion that I didn't know whether to laugh or cry. I felt like I had been let in on the world's best-kept secret. Everything was new and I loved it.

When I walked into Tenth with Harold, the atmosphere was much different than my mom's church, but that didn't matter to me. All I wanted was to hear about Jesus, which I would soon learn was the very thing the preachers at Tenth were eager to share. The pastor at the time was the legendary James Boice, who preached in the morning services. The main preacher at the evening service in those years was Dr. Philip Ryken. When Dr. Ryken preached, it felt like a glass of cold, purified water on a hot day for my soul. The clarity with which he explained the Bible left me refreshed and yet longing for more. Over time, I noticed that whenever he preached, he always presented the person and work of Jesus Christ, no matter what passage he was preaching on. Though I didn't know the phrase back then, this was my introduction to gospel-centered preaching, and I couldn't get enough of it.

At the same time, there were big cultural differences between me and most of the members at Tenth. Tenth was filled with upper class, suburban-raised, well-educated White Christians who seemed to love classical music. And here I was: a Black dude from a low-income household in West Philly who dropped out of college and was steeped in hip-hop culture. While I appreciated all the words and some of the tunes in the red Trinity Hymnal, singing the songs took some getting used to. In fact, there were many times when it literally hurt my throat to sing some of the hymns. It was like using a shoehorn to put on really tight shoes, but liking the shoes so much you're convinced they'll stretch out and become more comfortable one day.

In one sense, our worlds could not have been further apart. On the other hand, none of that mattered to me because I was among brothers and sisters in Christ, and we all united under the banner of Jesus Christ and Him crucified. Also, as one who had been socialized in hip-hop culture, neither Freedom nor Tenth was a perfect cultural fit for me. With my dreadlocks, baggy camouflage khakis, and Timberland boots, dear saints in both churches would often look at me, smiling, but with a slightly confused look on their faces. Over time, a pattern developed in my routine on Sundays. Freedom in the mornings, a nap in the afternoon, and Tenth in the evenings.

Hip-hop for Christ,
Just the Way the Lord Meant It

During this time, I continued performing in the Philly theater scene. Through an actor friend of mine, I met Phil, who was the director of SALT, a Christian street theater troupe. Phil and I hit it off immediately, and before long, I was performing with the group. We would hop into a van and travel up and down the East Coast, going straight to the corners of some of the roughest neighborhoods in cities like Baltimore, Washington, DC, and Newark. Our formula was simple: Gather a crowd by blasting some music. Perform evangelistic plays. Share the gospel at the end.

One of the plays we did had a scene in which the protagonist gets shot. We were performing the scene in Baltimore one day, and after the simulated shooting, a car screeched to a halt in the middle of the street. A man ran from the car in a frenzy, totally oblivious to the crowd that was gathered to watch the play. He knelt down where Phil was playing dead, saying, "Hey, man! You all right? You all right?" Someone from the crowd yelled, "Move, man! They're doing a play! Get out the way!" At that point, it hit him that he was interrupting a scene. The would-be Good Samaritan said, "My bad!" and sheepishly walked back to his car.

One of the other plays needed a character to rap during the finale. I told Phil that I rapped and could potentially write something for the part. This would be my first time writing a rap as a Christian. In middle school, I began writing rhymes, heavily influenced by my favorite lyricists at the time, like KRS-One, Rakim, Kool G Rap, Big Daddy Kane, and Slick Rick. In fact, I had aspired to a rap career before acting took my focus. Even after coming to Christ, though, I had no concept of "Christian hip-hop" until Phil played an album called *House of Representatives* by The Cross Movement. As I listened, I felt simultaneously joyful and perplexed as I tried to reconcile the conflicting dualities facing me. Musically, it was Wu-tang Clan, but lyrically it was Billy Graham. This shattered my previous categories concerning the relationship between Christianity and hip-hop culture. Based on the instrumental, my normal expectation would have been to hear about street life, drug sales, cars, etc. Instead, I was blown away as I heard:

> *Rise, shine! For the Light has come*
> *I count all things as dung*
> *Compared to the knowledge of God the Son . . .*
> *The Father brought us back, He devised a plan*

That His Son would bridge the gap between God and man
How else could the gospel be born
if His bodily form wasn't hostilely torn? This be the norm
Cruising heaven's highway representing Yahweh
The fly way, the do or die way
I won't hesitate to take my last breath
I'm ready to die 'cause I possess eternal life after death[1]

The boldness with which these brothers broadcasted the good news of Jesus was unlike anything I had ever heard in hip-hop. It was clear that they were motivated by something different than what I had heard all my life. I was used to rappers boasting about their money, cars, clothes, and skills. The Cross Movement was boasting about *God*. And as they did that, they made earnest appeals to their listeners concerning sin, death, the judgment to come, and the hope of eternal life through Jesus Christ. As a new convert, it brought me to tears to know that God had not overlooked the community I came from. He graciously sent hip-hop missionaries to speak the truth of the gospel to people just like me.

Jesus died for men—Who wants to live with Him?
You're gonna die too, friend, but you can live again
You see the love for the lost, He came down
You see the blood from the cross to the crown
Since the breakup, God and man can kiss and make up
If we take the incarnate ladder of Jacob
The Cross Movement here to wake ya
It's time to switch our praise from things made to the Maker[2]

Hearing this was the beginning of a paradigm shift for me. I

> # The music form that had indoctrinated me with anti-Christian views could be used to proclaim the same Christ I had rejected.

was starting to see that the music form that had indoctrinated me with anti-Christian views could actually be used to proclaim the same Christ I had rejected for so many years. Not only that, but in many ways, hip-hop was an ideal medium for that purpose.

Holy Culture

As I researched The Cross Movement online, I was pleasantly surprised to learn that they were based in Philly. Not only that, but they were throwing an album release party for one of their artists, William Branch, a.k.a. The Ambassador, for his debut album *Christology. Christology* took what I heard on The Cross Movement's other albums to another level. It was an integration of hip-hop and theology that transported the listener straight from the gritty pavements of the hood to the pristine hallways of the seminary.

> *Rough and tough without the "Afro Puff", it's the*
> *supernatural stuff*
> *All about His blood like we're Dracula*
> *With spectacular spiritual vernacular*
> *Like the concept of the hypostatic union coming smack at ya*
> *I know it's deep but when you peep you'll find it's dense*
> *Jesus, both God and Man, two hundred percent*[3]

The hypo-what?! I couldn't believe what I was hearing: music in my native cultural language that was God-glorifying, Christ-exalting, artistically pleasing, and intellectually stimulating with theological depth. I don't know if heaven has a radio station, but if it did, this would have to be on the playlist! *Christology* helped lay the groundwork for an entire community of emerging theo-centric hip-hop artists—myself included—who would build and expand on these ideas for the next decade.

The release party for *Christology* was being held at a church not far from where I lived. I went not knowing what to expect. When I walked into the church that night, I was amazed. There must have been a thousand people there, mostly young adults. I learned later that people had traveled from all over the country. I looked around, trying to process what I was seeing: baggy pants, fitted baseball caps, football and basketball jerseys, Timberland boots, hoodies and camouflage jackets, braids and dreadlocks.

Externally, this was without question a late '90s hip-hop crowd, looking like something out of *8 Mile*. But as different artists came to the stage, I saw something I had never seen at a hip-hop concert before: rappers who were rapping about Jesus and directing the attention of the crowd away from themselves to Christ. And the audience seemed to be more excited about Jesus than anything else, including the style of music we were enjoying.

When The Ambassador came out to perform his set, he was wearing a red and black basketball jersey, the colors of the Chicago Bulls. The number was Michael Jordan's iconic 23. But above the number 23, instead of "Bulls" it said "Psalm." I felt like I had stumbled into an alternate reality. Was all this happening right under my nose in my city at the same time that I was living in darkness just months before? As I absorbed all that was happening that night, I had an epiphany. At both Freedom and Tenth, though the saints loved the Lord and loved on me, treating me with nothing but kindness, I was in many ways a cultural outsider in both churches.

I was beginning to wonder how I could fit in as one who grew up in hip-hop culture. Would I be honoring Jesus more by wearing the suit that was given to me by a well-meaning brother at Freedom? Would I be a better Christian by cutting my hair? I learned an important lesson at the release party: Jesus wasn't calling me to abandon my culture . . . at least not the God-honoring aspects of it. Rather, He was calling me to leverage my culture for the glory of God. And now I was beginning to get a sense of what that could look like.

> Jesus wasn't calling me to abandon my culture . . . at least not the God-honoring aspects of it. He was calling me to leverage my culture for the glory of God.

Later that very night, I began putting pen to paper, seeking to write Christ-exalting lyrics. It was all starting to make sense to me. I had been called out of darkness into light, and God was calling me to proclaim His excellencies (1 Peter 2:9). And not just me. There was a thriving Christian hip-hop community right where I lived. I was marveling at the providence and wisdom of God.

Open Mic Night

A few weeks later, Harold and I were walking down South Street when we came across a new Christian bookstore and coffee shop.

Anyone who's familiar with South Street knows that it is one of the places that people come to in Philly with the express purpose to party. Then, it was a long strip lined with bars, palm reading shops, and sex-themed boutiques. It was not a place that you would expect to find a Christian presence. And yet, there was the bookstore. The owner was friendly and told us that there was a Bible study on Thursday nights led by a brother named Aaron. So the next week, I went to the study, and Aaron and I hit it off immediately.

Aaron was knowledgeable in the Scriptures. He was a hip-hop head with a pastor's heart. Outgoing and friendly, he was the type of person that people are naturally drawn to. We became friends, and eventually I told him I rapped and let him hear some of my lyrics. When Aaron's excited about something, it's not long before everyone around him knows about it. One night, Aaron asked me if I wanted to go to an open mic. When we got there, the man at the door said it was $20 to enter. I was immediately ready to leave. Aaron pointed to me and said, "I'll pay the $20. But if I do, can my man get on the open mic?" I was completely caught off guard, but Aaron's confidence in me was encouraging. The man at the door looked me up and down, noticed my baggy cargos, backpack, and dreads locked under a head wrap, and blurted out, "This is a *Christian* open mic, fellas." Aaron and I just looked at each other and laughed. Aaron assured him that we knew that. With a look of embarrassment on his face, the man said, "I'm sorry, y'all. Sure, he can sign up for the open mic."

When the time came, I got up and shared my lyrics. I don't remember being nervous at all. As I stepped onto the stage, the only thing on my mind was clearly communicating the beauty and saving power of Jesus. The crowd was familiar with some of the artists who went before me, even singing along with their lyrics. When I was introduced, I received some light courtesy applause, fitting for a polite Christian audience. They had no idea who I was. The live band that was playing that night surprised me when they started playing the instrumental to one of my favorite beats, "The Next Movement" by The Roots. It felt like the stars were aligned perfectly.

As I rapped, the audience seemed to hang on to my every word. By the end of the song, everyone was on their feet, clapping and shouting words of encouragement and affirmation. It was overwhelming. I learned later that the Philly Christian hip-hop scene was small enough that pretty much everyone knew each other. I'm sure many of them were wondering where I came from. It reminds me of when Jesus said that God can raise up children for Abraham out of stones if He so pleased. Here I was, a brand-new Christian, raised up from the stony sidewalks of West Philly to declare the works of God in hip-hop form.

At that point, I was just excited to rap about Jesus. It didn't matter who was there. But it just so happens that the entire Philly Christian hip-hop community was present that night, including The Cross Movement. This was my formal introduction to the scene. I made a number of connections that night, which eventually led to me getting a deal with a production company. Not long after that I began recording songs. Everything was moving very quickly, and it wasn't even something that I was chasing. It was like the Lord was going before me, flinging doors open at will and then guiding me through them. All that the Lord was doing in those early years was preparation for me to carve out my own lane and run hard in it for the glory of God.

Chapter 3

Lyrical Theology

In the months following the release party, I was so inspired that I began writing more Christ-centered rhymes. At Tenth Presbyterian, my young faith was beginning to become solidified. Essential truths of the Christian faith, such as the Trinity, the deity of Christ, the inerrancy of Scripture, salvation by grace alone, and justification by faith were beginning to crystallize. It was natural for me to begin incorporating the doctrinal truths I was learning into my lyrics.

Didactic Hip-Hop

I attended the evening services at Tenth for about a year. Eventually, I began attending morning services and became a member at the church. An organization called the Alliance of Confessing

Evangelicals (ACE) had a close association with Tenth. ACE was a ministry that produced numerous resources, such as books, sermon series, a bi-monthly magazine, and conferences, all focused on ACE's mission, which was to recover the biblical doctrines of the Protestant Reformation of the sixteenth century.

At one of the meetings of Tenth's young adult ministry, it was announced that ACE was looking for volunteers to do office work. Though it wasn't a paid position, volunteers would get a book for a certain number of hours worked. This is how I first started my theological library. I couldn't get enough of what I was reading. Books like *Knowing God* by J. I. Packer, *The Holiness of God* and *Chosen by God* by R. C. Sproul, *The Discipline of Grace* by Jerry Bridges, and *The Pleasures of God* by John Piper were formative for me. They were providing categories to help me understand what happened to me when I got saved. I knew that God had intervened in my life, stopped me from running hard in one direction, and turned me around, all by His power and mercy.

The hymns we were singing at Tenth gave me language to express what I knew to be true in the deepest part of my soul:

> *Long my imprisoned spirit lay*
> *Fast bound in sin and nature's night;*
> *Thine eye diffused a quickening ray,*
> *I woke, the dungeon flamed with light;*
> *My chains fell off, my heart was free;*
> *I rose, went forth, and followed Thee.*[1]

What I began to realize is that I had been chosen before the foundation of the world (Eph. 1:4) and that it was God's actions, not mine, that ultimately produced my salvation. I soon learned this biblical emphasis is the foundation of what's known as Reformed theology.

Because of my previous background in "Edutainment," the idea of using hip-hop to teach was not foreign to me. Also, as I began to learn about hymns, it struck me that hymn writers and hip-hop artists were using many of the same kinds of poetic devices. One thing that intrigued me with hip-hop compared to hymns was that I was able to fit many more words into the same amount of musical space. This meant that the potential transfer of information was much greater with hip-hop. I was and remain a firm believer that every rapper is a preacher. The only question is what your sermon's about. I loved the idea of crafting songs that taught biblical truth in memorable, catchy ways that could be used to help establish and undergird the faith of those who listened.

Through a mutual friend, I was introduced to Josh, who was the founder of an indie record label called Lamp Mode Recordings. Josh (aka DJ Essence) had recently committed to following Christ and wanted to use his label to spread the message of the gospel. We hit it off immediately. Josh is one of those people who has so many talents that after a while you begin to wonder, "Okay, what *can't* this guy do?"

In Lamp Mode's early years, Josh engineered all of my recording sessions, produced many of my songs, served as the DJ for my concerts, designed and ran the label's website, shot the promotional video content, and mixed and mastered the records for all of the artists on the label. As we worked on my first album, we spent a lot of time in prayer together. Often, when Josh would drop me off after a recording session, we would sit in his car parked outside of my house and cry out to God that He would use us to exalt the

name of Jesus and open up doors for us to share about Christ crucified and resurrected. Fifteen or so years later, I'm amazed that the
Lord is still answering many of the specific things we asked Him
for back then. My first album, which came out in 2005, was called
The Solus Christus Project. That title, Latin for "Christ Alone," was
my homage to one of the Five Solas of the Reformation.

We didn't see it as a formula at the time, but looking back, there
were clear distinctive elements to what we were doing at Lamp
Mode. We were basically taking the approach that we learned
from The Cross Movement and *Christology* and putting our own
Reformed spin on it. We began to incorporate sermon clips from
the preachers that we were learning from into the songs. In many
ways, our songs were pointing people beyond the songs themselves to the source material that drove the lyrical content. As I
thought through what we were doing, it seemed to me that the
phrase "lyrical theology" captured it well. So I coined the phrase
by using it in one of our songs.

Spread His Fame

The music that we were making was beginning to connect with
people. The internet and the digitalization of music was making
it easier to spread content worldwide. Requests began to come in
for us to do concerts across the US and even internationally. Additionally, other Christian hip-hop artists were putting out great
music around the same time. Artists like Flame, Lecrae, Trip Lee,
Da Truth, and others were popularizing Christian hip-hop. Lamp
Mode, along with artists like Christcentric, Curtis "Voice" Allen,
and others were making music that resonated in churches that

embraced Reformed theology. There was also a burgeoning movement developing known as "Young, Restless, and Reformed," a
phrase coined by Collin Hansen in his book of a similar title.[2]

Many within this mostly White movement embraced Christian
hip-hop. With catalysts like the formation of The Gospel Coalition, the Together for the Gospel conference, and Desiring God
ministries partnering with Christian hip-hop artists, an interesting
dynamic was created. The music of mostly Black Christians was
being promoted and embraced in circles that were predominantly
White.[3] It was encouraging that there seemed to be cross-cultural
unity, as the truth in the music transcended the cultural differences
between the artists and our new listeners. But there were a few incidents involving hip-hop music that revealed the cultural distance
that still existed and needed to be overcome.

The first occurred in 2006 when Curtis "Voice" Allen was invited to Bethlehem Baptist Church (pastored by John Piper at the
time) to perform his rap "Unstoppable" during one of the services.
A video of the performance got out, and it caused an uproar. A
number of Christians from Reformed and fundamentalist backgrounds expressed outrage that John Piper would allow rap music
in a church service. Some believed that the music style itself was
inherently dishonoring to God due to its secular origins. They saw
it as a form of worldly compromise. Others were more concerned
that it took place during a corporate worship service, which they
believed to be an inappropriate setting for that genre of music.
What no one could dispute, however, was that the actual words of
the song clearly pointed to God's saving power in the gospel.

The second happened a few years later when Christian rap artist
Propaganda released his song "Precious Puritans," which had lyrics
such as:

Hey Pastor you know it's hard for me when you quote
    Puritans
Oh, the precious Puritans
Have you not noticed our facial expressions?
One of bewilderment, and heartbreak, like "Not you too,
    Pastor"
You know they were chaplains on slave ships, right?
Would you quote Columbus to Cherokees?
Would you quote Cortez to Aztecs, even if they theology
    was good?
It just sings a blind privilege, wouldn't you agree?
Your precious Puritans[4]

This song also caused quite a stir in Reformed circles. Message boards exploded with vitriol and venom. Blog posts and think pieces were written by the dozens. Many thought Propaganda was being unfair by lumping all Puritans in together. Others came to Propaganda's defense and spoke of the importance of artistic license. At the time, many of us wondered if these were simply the natural growing pains that occur when two disparate cultures come together under the same roof. However, for many in the Christian hip-hop community, these disagreements revealed that it was time to take another look at our theological heroes from the past in order to better understand the men that we were reading, quoting, and recommending. What we found was eye-opening, to say the least.

BACKSTORY

Part Two

Chapter 4

Voices from the Past

"Yo, E, you gotta check this out! This dude is killing it!"

I couldn't hide my excitement as I, book in hand, approached my friend Eddie before our midweek Bible study. "This may be the best sermon I've ever read in my life! Well, top five at the very least." "Top five?" Eddie replied. "That's a bold statement, man." Undeterred, I said, "Yeah, yo. Listen to this line. It's old school language but check it out. You ready? Here it is.

There is an admirable conjunction of diverse excellencies in Jesus Christ.

"Yo! An admirable conjunction of diverse excellencies! That's crazy!" Eddie gave me a pound, smiled, and said, "What's that from? I gotta cop that!"

Eddie and I liked to share obscure books and quotes from

theologians with each other. The more unknown and obscure, the better as far as we were concerned. The quote was from a sermon by Jonathan Edwards, the eighteenth-century theologian, titled "The Excellency of Christ." To this day, it's one of the best things I've read about Jesus outside of Scripture. I handed the book to Eddie. "It's this sermon by Jonathan Edwards based on Revelation 5:5–6. It's talking about how Jesus is both the Lion and the Lamb and how He embodies both lion-like and lamb-like qualities at the same time! He's powerful like a lion and meek like a lamb. He's fully God and simultaneously dependent on God. He's perfect in glory yet perfect in humility."

My eyes lit up as I went on and on. But I could sense that Eddie wasn't tracking with me. He was just quietly staring at the cover of the book. I stopped mid-sentence. "What's wrong?" I asked. Eddie replied, "That's really dope, the things he's saying about Jesus and all. But I can't really rock with Edwards, man. You know he owned slaves, right?" I gave Eddie a knowing look. "Yeah, I know, man." Boy, did I know. I had wrestled with this knowledge for a few years at that point. I had been in numerous conversations with many Christians about this very thing.

Goin' Way Back

I don't remember how I first learned that Jonathan Edwards owned slaves. It had to have been when I was at Tenth Presbyterian. But I do remember hearing Bible teachers talk about it and basically dismissing it, saying that Edwards and others were "men of their day." That never sat well with me, because I also knew about men like Charles Spurgeon, John Newton, and William Wilberforce who opposed slavery. Not to mention Jonathan Edwards's own son, Jonathan Jr., was an abolitionist! All these men lived around the same time, read the same Bible as Edwards, and held to the same Reformed theology. Yet they came to conclusions that were completely antithetical to Edwards on the question of whether Christians should own slaves.

There is very little from the pen of Edwards himself regarding slavery, so gaining an exact understanding of his position centuries later requires at least some speculation. For other men like renowned evangelist George Whitfield, theologian J. L. Dagg, and James P. Boyce (the first president of The Southern Baptist Theological Seminary), there is more historical documentation of complicity in "racial" injustice. In some cases, they fully approved and participated in it.

I was at Tenth in 2004 when the Presbyterian Church in America (PCA) (the denomination of which Tenth was a part) held their General Assembly and released a statement on "racial" reconciliation that sent shockwaves through the denomination. In it, they acknowledged the Presbyterian Church's history of "pride," "complacency," and "complicity" in "national sin(s)" regarding "racism."[1] What was particularly striking was the directness and honesty with which the drafters of the document confronted the denomination's "racist" past:

> Both the Northern and Southern Presbyterian traditions,
> out of which most of the founding congregations of the
> PCA came, allowed extensive propagation of error and
> confusion on the matter of race. Through both verbal
> and written statements these errors were freely presented
> not only as pragmatic realities, but also as sanctioned

by Scripture: that certain races are inherently inferior to others; that slavery is justified; and that segregation based on race is justified, even if forced by law or institutionalized. The Southern Presbyterian tradition, in particular, publicly promulgated views of this nature to such an extent that they are inseparably identified with the teaching of the Presbyterian Church in the minds of many. Thus the Presbyterian Church failed to stand for biblical truth in these matters. Even where the official positions of the church did not reflect racist views, the silence of many in the church allowed the free expression of racist sentiments that were then perceived as the official position of the church.[2]

Just in case my Baptist friends are tempted, with arms folded, lips pursed, and pearls clutched, to wag their heads in disbelief concerning those racist Presbyterians, there is plenty of culpability to be passed around cross-denominationally. The Southern Baptist Convention (SBC), which happens to be the largest Protestant denomination in America, was literally "birthed out of a commitment to preserve and defend slavery."[3]

The current president of the Southern Baptist Theological Seminary, Albert Mohler Jr., pulled no punches when writing about the origins of the SBC:

> In fact, the SBC was not only founded by slaveholders; it was founded by men who held to an ideology of racial superiority and who bathed that ideology in scandalous theological argument . . . history proves slavery was the cause of [the SBC's] founding. Further, notable Southern

Baptists James P. Boyce and John Broadus, founders
of The Southern Baptist Theological Seminary, were
chaplains in the Confederate Army. Just a few months
ago I was reading a history of Greenville, South Carolina
when I came across a statement made by James P. Boyce,
my ultimate predecessor as president of SBTS. It was so
striking that I had to find a chair. This is a staggering moral
fact, and it raises many urgent questions.[4]

The more I began to look into the history of the church in the
US in general, and the Reformed church in particular, the more I
saw a church that, for many decades, was largely in step with the
sins of the surrounding culture regarding "race." This amounted to
a missed opportunity for the church to be a countercultural change
agent that displayed the transformative power of the gospel to em-
power Christians to love neighbor as self, regardless of "race" or
ethnicity. Of course, the problem of God's people conforming to
the surrounding godless culture is not a new one. There's a reason
why, two thousand years ago, the church in first century Rome was
given this command:

> Do not be conformed to this world, but be transformed by the
> renewal of your mind, that by testing you may discern what
> is the will of God, what is good and acceptable and perfect.
> (Rom. 12:2)

Long before the Holy Spirit inspired the apostle Paul to pen
the command in Romans 12:2, He inspired Moses to warn Israel
how they were to live when they entered the promised land after
the Exodus:

When you come into the land that the LORD your God is
giving you, you shall not learn to follow the abominable
practices of those nations. (Deut. 18:9)

Worldliness is a temptation in every age, including our own.
The only question is what form that worldliness takes. When we
see the sinful blind spots of Christians in previous generations,
love, which rejoices in the truth (1 Cor. 13:6), demands that we
acknowledge it and denounce it where necessary. But a spirit of
humility demands that we ask, as the disciples did, "Is it I, Lord?"
when Jesus predicted His betrayal (Matt. 26:22). Our first impulse should be, "Lord, where are my blind spots?", because we
definitely have them.

Why I Still Read Jonathan Edwards

When I spoke to Eddie, I didn't try to convince him that he should
read Jonathan Edwards. Eddie is a Black man who has experienced
the painful residue of "racism" in his immediate family's history, as
well as his own life. For him, the incompatibility of a professing
Christian owning slaves was too much for his own conscience to
overcome in order to enjoy the writings, no matter how Christ-
exalting they may be. I get it. When it comes to disputable matters,
the Bible says, "Each one should be fully convinced in his own
mind" (Rom. 14:5). There's too many other great writings out there
by other theologians who better reflected God's heart in this area
to insist that one must read Jonathan Edwards. So why do I read
him? There are two main reasons.

First, when it comes to Edwards and his views on slavery, there is a vacuum of information. In other words, what we don't know far outweighs what we do know. Whereas, when it comes to his writings, there are more than two dozen volumes, page after page of Christ-exalting, gospel-saturated, God-glorifying, theologically rich material. Now obviously, it's possible to write theologically correct things without knowing the God of the theology. But whenever there is a lack of information, we have the choice to fill in the gaps of our knowledge with either the best case or the worst case. As a Christian, part of hoping and believing all things (1 Cor. 13:7) is choosing the best case given the information that I have. For me, I have to weigh the many beautiful things I've read from him that point me to Jesus with the relatively little that I know about Edwards's slaveholding. And if there really is such a thing as the "aroma of Christ" (2 Cor. 2:14–15), my soul testifies that the writings of Edwards are permeated with the sweet-smelling fragrance of my precious Lord Jesus. When I read things like the following, my soul starts dancing like MC Hammer:

> Once, as I rid out into the woods for my health, *anno* 1737; and having lit from my horse in a retired place, as my manner commonly has been, to walk for divine contemplation and prayer; I had a view, that for me was extraordinary, of the glory of the Son of God; as mediator between God and man; and his wonderful, great, full, pure and sweet grace and love, and meek and gentle condescension. This grace that appeared so calm and sweet, appeared great above the heavens. The person of Christ appeared ineffably excellent, with an excellency great enough to swallow up all thought and conception. Which continued, as near as I can judge, about an hour;

63

which kept me, the bigger part of the time, in a flood of tears, and weeping aloud. I felt withal, an ardency of soul to be, what I know not otherwise how to express, emptied and annihilated; to lie in the dust, and to be full of Christ alone; to love him with a holy and pure love; to trust in him; to live upon him; to serve and follow him . . . and to be perfectly sanctified and made pure, with a divine and heavenly purity. I have several other times, had views very much of the same nature, and which have had the same effects.[5]

When I read that, it's like a neon sign in bright flashing red lights that this is a man who knows God. Not only am I struck by what I see when Edwards talks about God, but the way he speaks about himself in light of seeing God is just as illuminating:

My wickedness, as I am in myself, has long appeared to me perfectly ineffable, and swallowing up all thought and imagination; like an infinite deluge, or mountains over my head. I know not how to express better, what my sins appear to me to be, than by heaping infinite upon infinite . . . for this many years, with these expressions in my mind and in my mouth, "Infinite upon infinite. Infinite upon infinite!" When I look into my heart, and take a view of my wickedness, it looks like an abyss, infinitely deeper than hell. And it appears to me, that were it not for free grace . . . I should appear sunk down in my sins infinitely below hell itself. . . .

And yet. . . . It seems to me, my conviction of sin is exceeding small, and faint. . . . When I have had turns of weeping and crying for my sins, I thought I knew in the time of it, that my repentance was nothing to my sin.[6]

In passages like this, I see a man who not only knew his God, but who was well acquainted with his own wickedness and his need for grace, which is one of the first fruits of seeing God rightly (Isa. 6:5). I'm not here to declare with 100 percent certainty that Edwards was saved. I can't do that for anybody. God alone knows the heart and He's the perfect judge (Jer. 11:20). My point is that the writings of Jonathan Edwards bear the marks of someone who had a powerful encounter with the Lord. For many, the statement "he owned slaves" is enough to disqualify whoever the "he" is from the kingdom of God. (Personally, I'm slow to boot any professing Christian out of God's kingdom.) For me, that sentence alone is not enough to do it without additional context. For example, imagine the following scenario:

A White man named Charles Freeman was born in Connecticut in 1745. Charles had parents who were professing Christians and enslaved a Black married couple named Jesse and Mary, who played a large role in helping to raise Charles and his two younger siblings from childhood. Jesse and Mary were Christians and attended church with Charles and his family since Charles could remember. When Charles was 19, his parents died tragically on a trip to London. When it came time to settle his parents' affairs, Charles learned that Jesse and Mary were left to Charles in the will. (Because enslaved people were viewed as property, it was common for them to be passed down from one generation to the next.)

Charles had recently converted and he was a genuine believer who loved Jesus with all his heart. Even before he came to Christ, he hated the transatlantic slave trade and the institution of slavery. Though his parents treated Jesse and Mary relatively well, Charles still thought it was wrong that they were brought there against their will and were not being paid for their labor. He also hated the inhumanity he saw with the way many of his friends' parents treated those they enslaved. One night, Charles sat down with Jesse and Mary, who at that point were in their mid-forties. With tears streaming down his face, Charles apologized on behalf of his parents and told Jesse and Mary that he was willing to let them go free immediately, and though he knew it was very small compensation for all the work they had done, he was willing to split his share of his inheritance with them to help make up for some of what they lacked in wages all those years.

When Jesse and Mary thought about it, they realized that if they went free—as desirable as freedom is—their safety would immediately be jeopardized. They could have easily been kidnapped and sent to Mississippi or Alabama or even potentially separated and assigned to work on different plantations. Charles recognized this as well. Charles grabbed their hands, looked them in the eye, and said, "Mr. Jesse . . . Miss Mary . . . You are like family to me. More than that, you are my brother and sister in Christ. I actually learned more about Jesus from watching your example my whole life than I did from my own parents. I'm willing to have you in my home, but I will not treat you like slaves. Continue to do work around the house, and I will pay you as much as I can. I will also include you in my will, should anything happen to me. As far as the government is concerned, we have a master/slave relationship, but I don't see it that way at all. I love you and I pledge to treat you with the utmost dignity and respect for the rest of my life, regardless of what our surrounding culture says. And should you desire to be released at any moment, simply say the word and I won't hesitate to do whatever is necessary to safely and legally make that happen."

I'll stop this part of the fictional scenario there, because I'm not trying to do the magnanimous-White-savior-rescues-Black-people thing that we see in movies like *The Blind Side*, *The Help*, *Mississippi Burning*, and any number of offerings from Hollywood over the years. I hope you get my point. Let's assume Jesse and Mary agree to stay with Charles and end up living with the Freeman family for the rest of their lives. As far as recorded history is concerned, Charles Freeman was a slave owner. But with the gift of details and nuance rather than uncharitable caricature, we're able to see that the mere sentence, "He owned slaves" would not disqualify Charles from the kingdom at all. To be clear, I'm not saying that the hypothetical scenario I just mentioned applied to Edwards. When I told my wife this example, she said, "That's really charitable!" I agree. But that's the point. We simply don't know much about the circumstances of Edwards's slave-owning beyond "he owned slaves." For some, that's enough to disqualify him. Without more information, it's not enough for me to do the same.

There's another reason why I still read Jonathan Edwards. It's something that I learned from a sermon by Anthony Carter, pastor of East Point Church in Atlanta, Georgia. He preached it at the Miami Conference for African-American Pastors in 2001 and it was reprinted in his book *On Being Black and Reformed.*

In it, Carter references 1 Corinthians, chapter 3, where the apostle Paul is rebuking the church at Corinth for the way they were boasting in which teachers they followed:

> *For when one says, "I follow Paul," and another, "I follow Apollos," are you not being merely human?*
>
> *What then is Apollos? What is Paul? Servants through whom you believed, as the Lord assigned to each. (1 Cor. 3:4–5)*

Paul continues his argument at the end of the chapter by reminding the Corinthians that to focus on particular human instruments is to follow the world's wisdom, which is foolishness to God (v. 19). And he concludes with the powerful statement that there's no need for them to boast in different preachers and teachers because *all things belong to them.*

> *So let no one boast in men. For all things are yours, whether Paul or Apollos or Cephas or the world or life or death or the present or the future—all are yours, and you are Christ's, and Christ is God's. (1 Cor. 3:21–23)*

In other words, all faithful preachers and teachers are gifts from God *to* the church, to be used *by* the church, for the building up *of* the church. Paul is reminding them that they don't have to choose teachers like teenagers choose their favorite obscure bands and brag about how they knew about them long before they hit the mainstream. No Christian or group of Christians can corner the market on a particular teacher. If one's teaching is biblically sound and in accordance with "the faith that was once for all delivered to the saints" (Jude 3), then any saint is free to benefit from that teaching. In his sermon, Carter applied this point to teachers throughout church history:

All faithful preachers and teachers are gifts from God *to* the church, to be used *by* the church, for the building up *of* the church.

> So let us "take up and read." As Paul declared in 1 Corinthians 3:21, "All things are yours." All things are mine. Moses is mine. I can read Genesis and Exodus or I can put it down. It is mine. David is mine. I can read and reflect upon the Psalms at my convenience. Isaiah is mine. Jeremiah, Ezekiel and the prophets are mine. But not only that, Augustine and Athanasius are mine. Aquinas and Anselm are mine, too. Wycliffe is mine. Luther, Calvin, Zwingli and Knox are mine. Bunyan, Owen and Baxter are mine. Edwards, Whitfield and Wesley, along with Newton, Cowper, Watts and Toplady are all mine. Spurgeon is mine. Warfield is mine. Dorothy Sayers, Fanny Crosby, Thomas Dorsey are all mine. Campbell-Morgan and Lloyd-Jones are both mine. J. I. Packer, Machen, Murray, Graham, even MacArthur, Evans, Swindoll, as well as Berkhof, Boice, Piper, Sproul, Horton, Ellis, Nunes, Jones and all others who name the name of

Christ and have demonstrated their commitment to the faith once and for all delivered to the saints—all are mine, and I am Christ's and Christ is God's.[7]

Yes, it's true that Jonathan Edwards bought and owned slaves. Yes, I can totally understand if that makes it difficult for people of color in particular to read his writings. What's also true is that, according to 1 Corinthians 3, Edwards is mine. In His sovereignty, God gave Edwards a sharp theological mind and pronounced teaching gifts. I choose to accept and benefit from those gifts. I also choose to incorporate many of those ideas into rap songs to the glory of God, so that people who may not be able to hear it from him might hear it from me. Either way, may God be praised.

We're in the Building

One of the interesting things about Christian hip-hop is that God has used it to introduce many Black and Brown Christians to Reformed theology. In the early 2000s, we saw an influx of minorities into predominantly White churches, Bible colleges, and seminaries. What was surprising to many onlookers is the role that Christian hip-hop played in this movement. Minority Christians were hearing doctrinal truths unpacked in the music that caused them to desire to hear those same truths and emphases unpacked from Sunday to Sunday at their churches and day to day at their schools. Additionally, for the same reason, we began to see more minorities beginning to show up at theological conferences that were previously almost all White. The same held true for minorities speaking into the public discourse (articles, social media, blogs, etc.) in

Reformed circles where they previously had little input.

The tension this produced was painful at times, even if it was somewhat predictable. Like we saw with Curtis "Voice" Allen and "Precious Puritans," whenever you have a contrasting majority/minority cultural dynamic, there will inevitably be growing pains as the two cultures seek to understand each other and live together. Every culture has its blind spots. But if a culture is allowed to develop and crystallize over a long period of time with very little input from outside cultures, those blind spots can become set in place like concrete that is many cold winters removed from its nascent stages, when it was still workable wet cement.

> In a contrasting majority/minority cultural dynamic, there will inevitably be growing pains as the two cultures seek to understand each other and live together.

Marcos Ortega, a Latino pastor and graduate of Westminster Theological Seminary (a well-known Presbyterian Seminary in Philadelphia), addressed the inclusion of minorities in the Reformed tradition in his 2016 online article "To the Reformed World: Minorities Are Here to Stay."

> It was white writers and preachers that introduced me to the world of Reformed theology. And so I am indebted and thankful for the work of my white brothers and sisters in the Reformed world. I am not the only minority that was brought in to the Reformed tradition because of the work of my white brothers and sisters.

Well, now we're in the tradition. And there are things
in the tradition that have been neglected because of
the relatively monolithic worldview that the Reformed
tradition long held. This is not the fault of our white
brothers and sisters . . . We cannot expect to hold
worldviews that are naturally foreign to us because of
ethnicity, background, etc. But we can listen to those
other worldviews and together deepen our understanding
of one another in the love of Christ.

When minorities began to embrace the Reformed
tradition, we brought something in with us. And it is a
valuable thing. And it will require all of us to learn from
one another.[8]

Due to the increased presence of minorities, many within
Reformed churches were grappling with how to understand the
weaknesses and sins of historical heroes of the faith. It seemed
like an important conversation at the time. But in years to come,
those disagreements would feel almost petty compared to future
controversies. It would be the contrary responses to contemporary
events that would threaten to permanently fracture the unity between Black and White Christians in America on a grand scale. The
gloves were soon to come off and it was about to get ugly.

Chapter 5

Déjà Vu

déjà vu | ˌdäZHä ˈvo͞o |

    noun

    1. a feeling of having already experienced the present situation

    2. tedious familiarity

I remember the feeling I had as a teenager when I first saw the video of Rodney King's beating at the hands of the LAPD. King, a 25-year-old Black man, was beaten on March 3, 1991, after a high-speed chase that led to his arrest for drunk driving. But before he was arrested, he was surrounded by twenty-one White police officers, four of whom beat him with nightsticks and kicked him in the head and neck while the seventeen other police officers stood nearby and watched. Among the injuries that King suffered as a result of the beating were a broken leg, his eye swollen shut, lacerations on his face, and burn marks on his chest from the taser that was used on him. The only reason this is public knowledge today is because, unbeknownst to the LAPD, an amateur videographer named George Holliday was filming the incident from the balcony of his apartment across the street from where the beating took place.

I felt a number of emotions when I saw the video, but surprise was not one of them. By the time I was sixteen, the common sentiment among my family and friends was that police beat up Black people all the time. By this time, my mother and stepfather had divorced and we had moved back to predominantly Black West Philly from the predominantly White Northeast. Just a few years earlier, not far from where we lived in West Philly, police and members of a Black nationalist organization called MOVE had an armed standoff when police went to execute an arrest warrant. When members of MOVE refused to come out of the row home they occupied, the Philadelphia Police Department took an action that was unprecedented on US soil up to that point. A police helicopter dropped a bomb on the roof of the house in the middle of a crowded residential area, killing eleven people in the house, including five children. The fire that blazed in the aftermath of the bombing burned over sixty homes to the ground, destroying an entire city block and leaving over two hundred fifty people homeless.[1]

Events like this and the negative experiences of older relatives and family friends with the police—recounted in barber shops, at barbecues, and on basketball courts—were burned into my adolescent consciousness. My perception of the police growing up was that they were there to punish and smash rather than protect and serve. So when the Rodney King beating happened, the consensus among the Black people in my life and in communities around the country was, "They got them on tape! Finally, it's on camera! And everybody saw it. They're not gonna get away with it this time. Finally, somebody is gonna pay the price for doing what they've been doing to us all these years." In hindsight, that mindset was naive. I suppose that had we consulted our elders, who lived through Emmett Till (1955), Medgar Evers (1963), Fred Hampton (1969), and many other Black people being murdered without seeing their killers brought to justice, they would have cautioned us to dial back our assumption that justice would be served simply because it was caught on video.

On April 29, 1992, their fears were realized when a majority White jury acquitted the officers charged in King's beating. For the next six days, an ominous cloud of black smoke hovered over Los Angeles as many in the community took to the streets and rioted. My wife, Blair, grew up in South Central L.A. As her 11-year-old eyes peeked through the curtains at her living room window in those days, she vividly recalls Korean-American store owners on the roofs of their properties with guns, seeking to protect their businesses from rioters and looters. She recalls seeing Black store owners spray painting "Black owned" on their stores in hopes of avoiding being pillaged. She recalls seeing no police in the area for days, as people were left to their own devices, engrossed in sprees of lawlessness. And finally, she recalls military tanks cruising down her street when the National Guard was brought in to restore order to the city.

Seeing with New Eyes

When I came to Christ, among the things that needed to change in me was the way I viewed authority in general and police in particular. Before Christ, I had a general disdain for the police. Part of that was due to the experiences I mentioned earlier. Another part of it was that my sinful heart despised authority because I wanted to be autonomous. Simply put, I wanted to do as I pleased without having anyone interfere with annoyances like laws and rules. Ultimately, it was the law of God that I was resisting. But once my eyes were opened to see Jesus as the King of kings, I now recognized that I was His servant, which helped me to see that my former contempt for authority was rooted in my own pride. I also began to get to know police officers who were Christians. As a non-Christian, I never knew any cops personally. This changed immediately after I got saved. At my mom's church Freedom, one of the bi-vocational ministers was in law enforcement. He was a strong man with a gentle soul; a caring husband who loved the Lord, cherished his wife, and preached God's Word passionately. He was the first in a long line of godly men in my life who loved Jesus and were also police officers. As helpful as these living examples were, it was ultimately God's Word that began to re-shape my mind in terms of how I looked at the police:

> *Let every person be subject to the governing authorities.*
> *For there is no authority except from God, and those that*
> *exist have been instituted by God. Therefore whoever resists*
> *the authorities resists what God has appointed, and those*
> *who resist will incur judgment. (Rom. 13:1–2)*

Seeing that the government (and local police by extension) was instituted by God was a game changer for me. This gave me a whole new appreciation for the high calling that those in law enforcement have, in terms of promoting order in a fallen society. It also magnified how wicked it is when that God-given authority is abused and used as a means to terrorize people rather than to protect and serve them. This new perspective was fresh in my mind when I was asked to contribute an overview of the book of Romans in song form to a project called *13 Letters*, a rap album based on the Pauline epistles. When I rapped about Romans 13:1, I mentioned being mindful of God and submitting to the government. I can only imagine how pre-Christian Shai would have responded to hearing something like that! The Lord truly does make all things new.

Jesus Music

Speaking of a rap album based on the Pauline epistles, I would be remiss if I didn't mention that God was at work so powerfully in this era of Christian hip-hop that it was a normal thing for there to be rap albums based on the Pauline epistles! I'm convinced that when the story is told—either in future generations or perhaps the new heavens and new earth—that Christian hip-hop in the period of time c. 2002–2012 in America will be viewed as something of an awakening or revival similar to what God did with the Jesus Movement of the late 1960s/early '70s. The Jesus Movement began on the West Coast and drew many converts from '70s hippie culture. It birthed evangelical pillars like Calvary Chapel, which are still bearing much fruit over four decades later.

This time around, it involved converts from hip-hop culture, and time will tell what the Lord was up to in those years. What I have clearly seen is that there are numerous churches that have been planted, missionaries who have been sent out to foreign lands, seminary students who have been trained, pastors and teachers who have been raised up, Christian authors who have been published, Christian college professors who have been empowered, Christian educators who have been developed, and many other forms of Christian service that are directly influenced by Christian hip-hop. Surely God chooses the foolish things of the world to shame the wise (1 Cor. 1:27)!

And It Don't Stop

With the mostly White Young, Restless, and Reformed movement and the mostly Black Christian hip-hop movement coming together for various ministry partnerships, there was an added element of cross-cultural pollination that appeared to be an organic and spontaneous continuation of the "racial" reconciliation efforts forwarded by Christian organizations such as Promise Keepers in the 1990s. However, beginning in 2012, there was a steady stream of events, each of which increasingly revealed the presence of a great chasm between many Black and White Christians.

Trayvon Martin (2012)

On February 26, 2012, a 17-year-old Black youth named Trayvon Martin, after walking to a convenience store, was returning to the house of his father's fiancée, who lived in a gated community in Sanford, Florida. George Zimmerman, who was part of the neighborhood town watch, saw Martin walking and called the police on him, saying that he looked "suspicious."[2] Not long after the call to police, Zimmerman engaged Martin, and in the struggle that ensued between them, Martin was shot in the chest by Zimmerman and died on the scene. Zimmerman was later acquitted of second-degree murder and manslaughter charges.

Ferguson, MO Protests (2014)

On August 9, 2014, an 18-year-old Black man named Michael Brown Jr. was shot and killed by a White police officer named Darren Wilson. The next day, people in the city began a protest, which sparked several days of marches, violence, riots, and clashes with the police. On November 24, a grand jury made the decision to not indict Wilson, which set off another round of peaceful protests and riots as well.

Black Death Gone Viral (2014–2016)

With the ubiquity of cellphones with cameras, almost every person walking on the street now had the potential to become another George Holliday by capturing the latest Black person killed by police. Having lived through that time, it felt to me like another video was being released every other week. Eric Garner, Laquan McDonald, Freddie Gray, Sandra Bland, Walter Scott, and Philando Castile are just a few of the names of Black people who had encounters with police that were caught on camera. The circumstances of each case varied, but the common component of each incident is that Black people ended up dead following their interaction with law enforcement.

The Election of Donald Trump as US President (2016)

On November 8, 2016, businessman, reality television star, and Republican presidential nominee Donald Trump culminated his improbable campaign with a victory over Democratic nominee Hillary Clinton to become the 45th President of the United States, despite losing the popular vote. Many pundits believed that his victory was propelled by a reported 80 percent of people who identified in exit polls as White evangelicals casting their vote for him.[3]

The Killing of George Floyd

On May 25, 2020, George Floyd, a 46-year-old Black man in Minneapolis, Minnesota, was being arrested for allegedly using a counterfeit $20 bill at a convenience store. While he was being detained, bystanders recorded video of a White police officer named Derek Chauvin kneeling on Floyd's neck for several minutes. During that time, Floyd said he couldn't breathe, begged for his life, and called for his mother. By the time Chauvin released his knee from his neck, Floyd was unresponsive. Shortly afterward, Floyd was pronounced dead. The video went viral, sparking several months of protests throughout the US and around the world.

Different Worlds

As Christians publicly processed these things via social media, it quickly became clear that many Black and White Christians landed in completely different places with regard to each of these events. The effects were immediate and damaging. A March 2018 *New York Times* article titled "A Quiet Exodus: Why Black Worshipers

Are Leaving White Evangelical Churches" chronicled how these events, with the presidential election being the final straw, have caused many Black Christians to return to the Black churches they had left when they sought to unify with their White brothers and sisters years before.[4]

For many Black Christians in the Christian hip-hop community and beyond, there was a feeling of betrayal that many White Christians couldn't understand.

That feeling was something like this: Black Christians had made the effort to leave churches that were culturally familiar for the sake of the gospel and our theological like-mindedness. It had been an adjustment and a sacrifice for many Black Christians to worship in churches where the music style wasn't culturally familiar, the preaching style wasn't culturally familiar, the way community was done wasn't culturally familiar, and the social dynamics of the church itself weren't culturally familiar. But we were willing to do so because we had the gospel in common. And White Christians were happy to have us as long as we just rapped about the gospel and kept quiet about the things we talk about among ourselves all the time that deeply affect us. But the moment we expressed the pain we felt about "racial" injustice, many White Christians were quick to dismiss us, rebuke us, or silently ignore us. If this was how we were going to be treated, we'd rather go back to the churches where the theological agreement may not have been as great, but at least we knew we'd be cared for, heard, and understood.

For many White Christians, there was confusion about why Black Christians were so affected by these killings, many of which involved people with criminal backgrounds. Especially because the way Black Christians processed the shootings seemed as if they were buying into the narrative of the liberal media, which does everything it can to stoke the flames of "racial" tension and make everything about "race" when it's not.

Pastor Bob Bixby captured the divergent perspectives of many White and Black Christians well in his 2014 article, "The Gospel in Black and White: A Missiological Perspective on Ferguson":

> Why is the common ground so elusive? Why is it that sincere Christians, white and black, instinctively analyze a crisis like Ferguson along color lines when they both love the same Lord? Many white Christians sincerely wonder how any sincere black Christian can take offense at their calls for delayed judgement "until all the facts are out" while seemingly ignoring the alleged bad behavior of the victim that put him into conflict with a police officer in the first place. And many black Christians wonder how any sincere white Christian cannot see the obvious problem of prejudice and white-on-black abuse of authority that exacerbates tension and escalates any confrontation between black youth and white authority in ways that are manifestly unfair. And so the churches meet separately.[5]

Bixby goes on to explain that the common ground will remain elusive until one or both groups are willing to enter into the other's world in order to develop the empathy that nurtures the pursuit of true understanding. I think Bixby is right. But there was one question that kept nagging me as I read history and noticed what can only properly be called a failure on the part of Reformed theologians to address "racism" in their work. As I perused the systematic theologies of Reformed giants, particularly Americans, it's striking how little there is about the sin of "racism," considering how that has been a major issue in our country for so long. Why is that? Is there something about Reformed theology that makes its adherents blind to the issue of "racial" injustice? In order to begin seeking an answer to that question, we'll need to go back to the Protestant Reformation and see what it was all about.

Chapter 6

Is Martin Luther My Homeboy?

Before I was a Christian, I don't recall ever hearing about Martin Luther. If the others in my Sunday school class at Tenth Presbyterian could have eavesdropped on my thoughts when I first heard him mentioned, I'm sure it would have been pure comedy.

> *Okay . . . Here we go . . . I keep hearing about this "Protestant Reformation" thing and how important it was . . . can't wait to find out what it was all about . . . wait a second . . . Martin Luther King was German!?!? What in the world? I never heard anything about that . . . and what's this about him being a monk? He was a Baptist preacher! That ain't no monk! . . . Should I raise my hand and say something? . . . Oh, wait, different guy . . . got it.*

As I considered the stained history of the Reformed church in America regarding "race," one recurring question for me was this: is there something inherent within the doctrines of Reformed theology that produces a blindness to "racial" injustice and ethnic oppression? In order to answer this, let's first take a look at the Protestant Reformation.

Time to Spark the Revolution

In seeking to identify the seminal moment that launched the Reformation, many historians point to October 31, 1517, the date that German monk Martin Luther (1483–1546) is said to have posted his 95 Theses on the door of a church in Wittenberg. At the time, the Roman Catholic church had a widespread practice of selling indulgences. Indulgences were basically a get-out-of-jail-free card from purgatory, which was believed to be a kind of holding cell after death where people's sins needed to be cleansed before they could go to heaven. Neither purgatory nor indulgences can be found in the Bible, and the fact that those teachings were so widely accepted and propagated in Luther's day indicates how far the Roman Catholic Church had strayed from biblical orthodoxy. When Luther posted his theses, he was calling the church back to the Bible, rather than the pope or the church, as the ultimate authority in matters of life and doctrine.

Aided by the invention of the printing press, Luther's writings "went viral" throughout Europe. In God's providence, four other church leaders—French pastor and theologian John Calvin (1509–1564), Swiss pastor Huldrych Zwingli (1484–1531), Scottish pastor John Knox (c. 1514–1572), and English scholar

William Tyndale (1494–1536) combined with Luther to form a kind of theological Voltron. A seismic religious revolution occurred, producing innumerable ripple effects that can be felt to this day. Michael Reeves and Tim Chester point this out in their book, *Why the Reformation Still Matters*:

> Five hundred years on, does the Reformation still matter? It matters because this is our story. If you are Anglican, Baptist, Brethren, Congregational, Independent, Lutheran, Mennonite, Methodist, Pentecostal, Presbyterian, or Reformed, then these are your roots. Your history can be traced back to these events five hundred years ago.[1]

So what were the Reformers aiming to address in their writing, preaching, and teaching concerning the church? The answer can be found in what became known as the Five Solas of the Reformation. In more recent years, the Cambridge Declaration of 1996 was written by a group of evangelical pastors and scholars who were seeking to reclaim these Reformation emphases. They restated the Five Solas, incorporating a series of reaffirmations. I'll be using excerpts from that statement as I walk through the Five Solas.

1. A Right View of the Bible (Sola Scriptura)

At the time of the Reformation, the pope and the church's tradition were considered to be on the same level as Scripture. In the Catechism of the Catholic Church, under point 95, it says:

> It is clear therefore that, in the supremely wise arrangement of God, sacred Tradition, Sacred Scripture and the

Magisterium of the Church [the pope and the bishops in communion with him] are so connected and associated that one of them cannot stand without the others.[2]

When Martin Luther was brought before Holy Roman Emperor Charles V and interrogated concerning whether or not he would recant his teachings, Luther famously replied,

> Unless I am convicted of error by the testimony of Scriptures or (since I put no trust in the unsupported authority of Pope or of councils, since it is plain that they have often erred and often contradicted themselves) by manifest reasoning I stand convicted by the Scriptures to which I have appealed, and my conscience is taken captive by God's word, I cannot and will not recant anything, for to act against our conscience is neither safe for us, nor open to us. On this I take my stand. I can do no other. God help me. Amen.[3]

With Sola Scriptura ("Scripture alone" in Latin), the Reformers were affirming that the Bible is "the sole source of written divine revelation, which alone can bind the conscience. The Bible alone teaches all that is necessary for our salvation from sin and is the standard by which all Christian behavior must be measured."[4] God's Word has everything that we need for life and godliness (2 Peter 1:3). Whenever we veer from the Scriptures, error and confusion are inevitable. The hope and thrust of Sola Scriptura was that the average Christian would no longer be solely reliant on the professional clergy to tell them what the Bible said and meant, but rather, that every Spirit-filled Christian could read, understand,

and study the Bible for themselves. This is not to negate the role of pastors, who are gifts from God to His church (Eph. 4:11). But whether pastor, pope, or plumber, we all must bow the knee to the Lord and submit to the Scriptures as our ultimate authority.

2. A Right View of Salvation (Sola Gratia, Sola Fide)

An overestimation of humanity's spiritual ability has always coincided with an underestimation of the holiness of God and human sinfulness. When the Holy Spirit inspired the Scriptures, flattering the fallen human ego was not on His agenda. It is only as we move away from the teaching of the Bible that we rise in our esteem of our own moral performance. In Romans 3:10–12, we see the divine perspective on human righteousness:

> *"None is righteous, no, not one;*
> *no one understands;*
> *no one seeks for God.*
> *All have turned aside; together they have become worthless;*
> *no one does good,*
> *not even one."*

By the time of the Reformation, it was common belief that the way to true piety was to enter the monastery to live that "monk life." The problem with that is evident: wherever you go, there you are. No monk or nun ever found a way to leave their sinful hearts at the door of the monastery (Jer. 17:9). Luther discovered this for himself, having such an awareness of his sinfulness and guilt before God that he is said to have spent hours a day in confession. I'm sure the priest got tired of seeing him! What Luther eventually learned is that it wasn't *his* righteousness that made him right with God, but the righteousness of Christ, which comes through faith. If he was ever going to be accepted by God, Luther knew that God Himself had to take the initiative, apart from any human work or effort. Our choosing God is the consequence, rather than the cause, of God's choosing us. This is the meaning of Sola Gratia (Latin for "grace alone"): "In salvation we are rescued from God's wrath by his grace alone. It is the supernatural work of the Holy Spirit that brings us to Christ by releasing us from our bondage to sin and raising us from spiritual death to spiritual life."[5]

Sola Fide (Latin for "faith alone") speaks to how we receive the gift of God's grace in salvation. In Luther's day, the Roman Catholic church taught the idea of an infused grace that could just as easily be lost as it was gained. And once lost, it was up to the de-graced person to gain it back through performing various church-sanctioned rituals and exercises. It was basically the see-saw version of the Christian life, not much different than what we see in modern Christian camps where guilt-laden teens repeatedly go up to altar calls to get "re-saved" each summer. Luther was trapped under this cycle of guilt and condemnation until he meditated on a passage from Romans chapter 1.

> For I am not ashamed of the gospel, for it is the power of God for salvation to everyone who believes, to the Jew first and also to the Greek. For in it the righteousness of God is revealed from faith for faith, as it is written, "The righteous shall live by faith." (Rom. 1:16–17)

After many years of struggling with the concept of a holy God and its implications for him, Luther recognized that verse 17 was teaching that the righteousness of God is imputed or credited once for all to the accounts of those who believe. This is the glorious doctrine of justification by faith alone, that God declares sinners to be righteous by faith (Rom. 4:4–5). When Luther discovered this, he said, "Here I felt that I was altogether born again and had entered paradise itself through open gates."[6]

Many theologians have referred to justification by grace alone through faith alone as the *material cause* of the Reformation; in other words, it's at the very heart of the Reformation. This is because it's also at the heart of what it means to be saved. God inspired an entire book of the Bible (Romans) that is completely structured around this doctrine. Every chapter deals with either the need for, the explanation of, or the implications of justification. Addressing this point, the writers of the Cambridge Declaration wrote: "We reaffirm that justification is by grace alone through faith alone because of Christ alone. In justification Christ's righteousness is imputed to us as the only possible satisfaction of God's perfect justice."[7]

3. A Right View of Christ (Solus Christus)

The Bible is very clear that "There is one mediator between God and men, the man Christ Jesus" (1 Tim. 2:5). But because of their departure from Sola Scriptura, the church at the time of the Reformation had sadly (and blasphemously) elevated Mary, other saints, and priests to the role of de facto mediators. This is nowhere to be found in the Bible. The Reformers emphasized that our salvation was achieved by no one other than Jesus Christ (Solus Christus, Latin for "Christ alone").

The writers of the Cambridge Declaration referred to this when they wrote: "We reaffirm that our salvation is accomplished by the mediatorial work of the historical Christ alone. His sinless life and substitutionary atonement alone are sufficient for our justification and reconciliation to the Father."[8]

4. A Right View of God (Soli Deo Gloria)

By the time the apostle Paul got to the end of Romans 11, after considering the redemptive plan of God in justifying sinners through faith in Christ along with its global ramifications, his only alternative at that point was to explode into doxological praise beginning in verse 33. When Paul got to verse 36, he concluded this section with a profound truth stated very simply:

> For from him and through him and to him are all things. To him be glory forever. Amen. (Rom. 11:36)

Amen indeed. God has set up salvation in such a way that He alone would get all the glory (Soli Deo Gloria, Latin for "glory to God alone)." Though this is listed last here, it's really the point from which everything else springs. The Reformation was about God being seen for what He really is—absolute in His majesty, supremacy, and glory. We really only have two options when it comes to our view of salvation: we will either elevate man and diminish God, or we will elevate God and diminish man. The fallen human tendency is to elevate man. This was the case in biblical times. It's certainly true today. And it was true at the time of the Reformation. The emphasis in the Five Solas is on the work of God alone, and what He has done to save His people from their sins. The prophet Isaiah wrote about how the God of the Bible saves:

> The LORD saw it, and it displeased him
>   that there was no justice.

He saw that there was no man,
and wondered that there was no one to intercede;
then his own arm brought him salvation,
and his righteousness upheld him. (Isa. 59:15b–16)

As it was prophesied in Isaiah, so it has always been. God saves without any outside assistance whatsoever. As the church moms say, "He's God all by Himself. And He don't need nobody else." Contrary to popular opinion, the saying "God helps those who help themselves" is not in the Bible. Benjamin Franklin said it, and last I checked, he was not an apostle. God helps the helpless. He helps the weak and the feeble, not the strong. He helps those who recognize that apart from Him, they can do nothing (John 15:5). Jonah recognized this. That's why he said, "Salvation belongs to the LORD!" (Jonah 2:9).

Upon reflecting on this point, the writers of the Cambridge Declaration wrote: "We reaffirm that because salvation is of God and has been accomplished by God, it is for God's glory and that we must glorify him always. We must live our entire lives before the face of God, under the authority of God and for his glory alone."[9]

When I was writing my album *The Attributes of God,* in which each song focused on a different aspect of God's character, I needed an "umbrella" song that would sum up the entire album. It was a daunting task, and the only thing I could think to write was a song called "The Glory of God" with each verse ending with a paraphrase of Romans 11:36. But even in the song itself, I had to acknowledge that human language is insufficient to properly describe a God who is incomprehensible.

Imagine it, I can't explain the half of it
Our brains can't even fathom it and language is inadequate
To characterize the Lord on the throne, with spiritual eyes,
His story is known
From Him and through Him and to Him is everything
Surely to God be the glory alone! [10]

So, Is It the Doctrine?

As I briefly survey the Five Solas, I see nothing inherent in the teaching itself that would lead to blind spots concerning "racial" injustice. As was noted above by Michael Reeves and Tim Chester, the reclamation of the gospel in the Reformation was the foundation for many major evangelical denominations—denominations that contain a wide range of ethnicities and cultures. Reformation theology is simply "Big God Theology." [11] True Christians all over the world in every era of church history have acknowledged that God, through the finished work of Christ, sovereignly saves His people by grace through faith apart from works of the law—even those who may not be consciously aware of the theological categories birthed from the Reformation.

The Reformation was not an invention, but a recovery.

Some have criticized Reformed theology as being inherently Eurocentric because of where the Reformation began. The first problem with that line of thinking is that the Reformers were clearly leaning on the teachings of African theologian Augustine of Hippo (354–430). The second and bigger problem is that the Old and New Testaments, a collection of Middle Eastern documents, clearly and repeatedly teach what is outlined in the Five Solas. The Reformation was not an invention, but a recovery. However, there is a quiet elephant that has been sitting patiently in a corner of this room that needs to be discussed.

Martin Luther's Anti-Semitic Writings

In 1543, just three years before his death, Martin Luther wrote a shocking treatise called *The Jews and Their Lies*. What he says in it about Jews is wicked, point blank. He advocates violence against them, says they should be forced into slavery, and uses all kinds of vulgar scatological references to demean and belittle them. And this was only one of a number of his anti-Semitic writings. The writings were so hateful they were actually used by Nazis as propaganda during the Holocaust. It's horrible. And it's far removed from the heart of God speaking through the apostle Paul, who wrote this in the book that Luther had translated into German from Greek and most likely had memorized:

> *I am speaking the truth in Christ—I am not lying; my conscience bears me witness in the Holy Spirit—that I have great sorrow and unceasing anguish in my heart. For I could wish that I myself were accursed and cut off from Christ for the sake of my brothers, my kinsmen according to the flesh. They are Israelites, and to them belong the adoption, the glory, the covenants, the giving of the law, the worship, and the promises. To them belong the patriarchs, and from their race, according to the flesh, is the Christ, who is God over all, blessed forever. Amen. (Rom. 9:1–5)*

The apostle Paul, a Jew himself, loved the Jewish people. As much as many of them hated Christ, it brought Paul sorrow to see them perishing. So much so, that he would have traded places with them if that were possible. He wanted to see them saved, not murdered. I can only hope that Martin Luther repented of his hateful attitude toward the Jews. The Lord knows. But what I can say is that it definitely wasn't the doctrine contained in the Five Solas that fueled his anti-Semitism. The Scriptures are largely written about, by, and for Jewish people. Our Savior is Jewish. God chose the Jewish people out of all nations to be His treasured possession (Deut. 7:6–7). Depending on how you read Romans 11, God will at some future point bring many Jewish people back to embrace their Messiah. Anti-Semitic hate speech is not only contrary to the doctrines of the Reformation, it's contrary to the fundamental command from God to love your neighbor as yourself (Mark 12:31).

> I'm not going to blame Reformation teaching for the sin of Martin Luther or Jonathan Edwards any more than I would blame the teachings of the New Testament when I disobey God.

When Martin Luther sinned in this way, he was contradicting the doctrine he espoused, not adhering to it. The same can be said for each and every one of us when we sin. I'm not going to blame Reformation teaching for the sin of Martin Luther or Jonathan Edwards any more than I would blame the teachings of the New Testament when I disobey God. So if it's not the teaching causing the blind spot, what is it? This is a question I've wrestled with for years. I still don't have a definitive answer, but I do have a theory.

The Low End Theory[12]

I mentioned the printing press earlier and how that helped to propel the spread of the Reformation throughout Europe. One important consideration is that literacy rates were very low back then. Historians estimate that less than 10 percent of the European population was literate when the Reformation began. At that time, literacy was tied to class. Wealth and access to education were the primary determinants of literacy. In other words, the poor, or the "low end" of society, were at a disadvantage when it came to interacting with both the Bible and the religious writings that were being disseminated throughout the culture at the time. While the Reformation was a big catalyst in improving European literacy rates in the coming centuries, the primary exchange of ideas was happening among the literate, who were the elite of society, i.e., those in power. Later on, in America, we know that it was against the law for a slave to even be taught how to read. So here's my theory, which is really a series of questions:

1. Could it be that, due to the literacy issue, Reformed theology as we know it was something that for centuries was primarily embraced and most precisely articulated by wealthy and powerful Christians?
2. If that is the case—and history tells us that those in power generally tend to do what they can to stay in

power and maintain the status quo—could that be the reason why there appears to have been so little written by the American descendants of the Reformation on slavery, the biggest social problem of their day?

3. Could it be that Christians on the "low end," both in Europe and America, didn't have the means, numbers, or resources to meaningfully engage and challenge the Christian elites on what it looks like to apply the gospel in the realm of oppression/injustice toward the poor?

I don't have the answers to these questions, but as a descendant of those on the "low end," I have my suspicions.

One Last Latin Phrase

There is no question in my mind that God was powerfully at work in the Protestant Reformation, despite the sinfulness of its leaders. (If the Bible and experience teach us anything, it's that if God is going to work with *anybody*, it's going to have to be "despite their sinfulness.") And yet American history has painfully shown us that embracing Reformed theology didn't automatically lead to the church being distinct from the world in how it dealt with the issue of "race."

One motto that sprung from the Reformation era is the notion of "semper reformanda" or "always being reformed." The idea was that the Protestant Reformation wasn't an end, but a crucial point in a continuing journey. As our forebears put it, "the church is always in need of being reformed according to the Word of God."[13]

As important as it was for the church to recover essential doctrines concerning salvation, the church, both individually and corporately, is still continually being sanctified by the Spirit of God. Therefore, until the return of Christ, there will always be a need for the church to grow in how she lives out the implications of the gospel. As I look over both the historical and present-day landscape regarding ethnic unity in the church, it's plain as day to see. We need a new Reformation.

HIS
STO
RY

Part
Three

Chapter 7

Ethnicity and the Fall

One of the sad byproducts of the fall of humanity into sin has been the ubiquitous nature of ethnic strife. Our sin nature has made us experts at identifying differences between us and our fellow image bearers, and then finding creative ways to rationalize using those differences as justification to mock, marginalize, maim, and murder. Every elementary schoolyard bears witness to our innate ability to target and ostracize people we perceive as "other" from us. History is replete with atrocities so grim that it requires phrases such as "ethnic cleansing" to be registered into the human lexicon. Whether it's Europeans and Africans in the transatlantic slave trade, Turks and Armenians in World War I, Germans and Jews in World War II, Serbs and Bosnian Muslims in the former Yugoslavia, or Hutus and Tutsis in Rwanda, the blood of the victims of ethnic genocide has cried out from the ground for many centuries. While Christians can grieve at the above examples and identify those things as heinous and offensive to a holy God, our twofold indwelling of sin and the Holy Spirit causes us to seek out more sanctified ways to bring our contributions to the ethnic strife potluck.

For us, it's probably not hacking someone to death with a machete or leading people to a gas chamber, but it might be tearing someone down with our words on social media or laughing at the "racist" joke our coworker told us. We pat ourselves on the back for never having shed innocent blood over someone's ethnicity, while at the same time, we look down with haughty eyes upon certain ethnicities, failing to discern that both things are abominations in God's sight (Prov. 6:16–17). The household of faith, past and present, is not immune to bad fruit in the realm of "race." It almost feels inevitable that the church's public discourse on this subject will lead to discord. Wretched men and women that we are! Who will rescue us from these bodies of death? The good news is that God has not left us on our own to try to figure this out. God has spoken loudly and repeatedly, if only we had eyes to see and ears to hear.

We Got Everything We Need

In our last chapter, we spoke about the Reformation principle of Sola Scriptura, that the Bible is the only ultimate authority to govern the faith and practice of Christians. Implicit within this idea of the *authority* of Scripture is that the Scriptures are also *sufficient* for our faith and practice as well. So when it comes to the issue of "race," we should look to the Bible, rather than the culture, to guide how we think about it. I can't stress this enough. Far too often, when Christians discuss this topic in the public square, the talking points sound like they come more from our favorite news channels, podcasts, and social media influencers than the Bible. This should not be. If we are going to make any progress in these discussions, the Bible must have first and final say on this topic.

We will neither honor the Lord nor make progress toward unity unless Christians on all sides of the "race" issue are willing to have our own perspectives enlightened by, challenged by, corrected by, and even rebuked by the Bible.

When it comes to the issue of "race," we should look to the Bible, rather than the culture, to guide how we think about it.

The Bible speaks to this issue. That should not be a controversial statement. However, if we were to gauge how much the Bible addresses "race" and "racism" based on the teaching of leading Reformed theologians in the last one hundred years, it would be hard to blame their readers for thinking Scripture was ambiguous at best and silent at worst when it comes to "race." J. Daniel Hays picks up on this in his book *From Every People and Nation: A Biblical Theology of Race*:

> Indeed, evangelical biblical and theological scholarship has continued to remain nearly silent on this issue, even though the indications of the scope of the problem are obvious. Few of our theological training institutions address the race issue, which is rather strange, considering the scale of the problem. Indeed, the traditional

Systematic Theologies used for most of the twentieth century did not address the race issue at all. Often these volumes had entire chapters devoted to philosophical and biblical discussions of "Anthropology" (the study of the nature of humankind), but they failed to address one of the central anthropological problems within the Church today. Likewise they contained entire chapters on "Ecclesiology" (the study of the Church), but did not address the major division in Church life today.[1]

Why is this important topic missing from the works that we rightly esteem for their theological precision in other areas? I think it goes back to my "low end theory" from the last chapter. It's not that this hasn't been talked about in the church at all. Black theologians and pastors have been talking about "race" and "racism" in our churches and writings since slavery.[2]

It's White theologians who have largely neglected this subject. I'm sure part of it is due to segregation. It's difficult to feel like an issue is important, let alone urgent, if you're purposely removed from the people most affected by it. Part of it may have been institutional pressure. I can only imagine how the trustees at a southern Presbyterian or Baptist seminary in the 1930s and 1940s would have responded had one of their professors advocated for the equality of Black people and the Bible's blessing on "interracial" marriage in his systematic theology! Whatever the issue was, one thing is certain: their silence was not because the Bible doesn't speak on it. So let's dive in.

Defining Our Terms

Up to this point, I've used the term "race" without defining it. That has been intentional. "Race" is a word that is used often in our culture with a shared assumed meaning. Historically, in America, it usually has been tied to physical traits like skin color, facial features, and hair texture. Due to the volatile history of relationships between Black and White people in America, along with politicization, "race" has become a hot-button issue that can reflexively provoke strong emotional responses. I need to say from the outset that I recognize that the struggle for unity among Christians is much broader than Black and White people in America.

To my Asian, Latino, Indian, Middle Eastern, African, Caribbean brothers and sisters, and brothers and sisters of other nationalities: I see you. I've given precedence to the American Black/White dynamic because of its unique history, along with the way Christianity has factored into that story. I also believe that addressing the Black/White American relationship could be paradigmatic for how other groups of Christians may chart a path forward toward greater unity. As I've used the term so far, I've given the reader the license to import whatever meaning "race" had when they first opened the book. Moving forward, however, I'm going to be more precise in how I speak about it.

Ethnicity Rather Than "Race"

As Christians, it's important for us to avoid allowing the world to dictate our agenda and how we talk about things. So far, I've been using "race" and ethnicity interchangeably. But categorically, I believe *ethnicity* is the proper term for Christians to adopt as we engage on this subject. Usually, in our context, when people mention "race," they're actually talking about ethnicity. The problem with the idea of "race" as it has been used historically is that it was socially constructed as a way to justify slavery in America. First, "race" has been shown to have no scientific basis whatsoever. Biologically speaking, the differences between human beings of different skin colors and hair textures are negligible at best.[3] More significantly, "race" is not a biblical category. Ethnicity, on the other hand, does have a biblical basis. So what is ethnicity? Most dictionaries say something to the effect of: "The fact or state of belonging to a social group that has a common national or cultural tradition."[4]

Here's how a contemporary cultural anthropology textbook defines ethnicity:

> In essence, an ethnic group is a named social category of people based on perceptions of shared social experience or one's ancestors' experiences. Members of the ethnic group see themselves as sharing cultural traditions and history that distinguish them from other groups.[5]

To put it simply, an ethnicity is a group of people who are identified with each other based on particular similarities. Those similarities are most often cultural, but they can also be physical or a combination of the two. So for example, African Americans are a distinct ethnicity. There is a shared language, a shared history, a shared ancestry, and shared cultural reference points, along with shared physical features. On the other hand, certain Caribbean peoples of African descent may share some of the same physical features as African Americans, but properly speaking, they're a different ethnicity due to a different shared language, history, homeland, and cultural reference points. This is why it's common for Africans around the world to struggle with understanding particular aspects of the relationship between Black and White people in America, even if they can draw some inferences based on their own reference points. It's evident that two people can have similar physical features and yet be a completely different ethnicity. So why do I say that ethnicity is a more biblical idea?

Ethnicity in the Bible

There's an important Greek word in the Bible that I want to draw your attention to. That word is "ethnos" (or a related term, ethne'). The root of that word is related to the English word ethnic.

> éthnos (from ethō, "forming a custom, culture") – properly, people joined by practicing similar customs or common culture; nation(s), usually referring to unbelieving Gentiles (non-Jews)[6]

Ethnos is often used to refer to everyone outside of the Jews. When we see "nations" in the Septuagint (LXX) (the oldest known copy of the Greek Old Testament), or "Gentiles" in the New Testament, ethnos is usually the term behind that word, appearing over four hundred times in the LXX and over one hundred times in the New Testament. When it appears, it is referring to distinct people groups, and that distinction is cultural. This is seen throughout the Old Testament. God is not just the God of Israel, but He rules over the nations.

All the ends of the earth shall remember
and turn to the LORD,
*and all the families of the **nations** [ethnos in the LXX]*
shall worship before you. (Ps. 22:27)

*All the **nations** [ethnos in the LXX] you have made shall come*
and worship before you, O LORD,
and shall glorify your name. (Ps. 86:9)

So where did these nations, or ethnicities, come from? After
Adam and Eve were booted from the garden of Eden for eating
the forbidden fruit, it didn't take long for the effects of their sin to
infect the entirety of their progeny. In Genesis 6:5, it says:

The LORD *saw that the wickedness of man was great in the*
earth, and that every intention of the thoughts of his heart
was only evil continually. (Gen. 6:5)

The consequence of this wickedness was God's judgment with
the flood in the days of Noah, which wiped out everyone on earth
except for Noah's family. In Genesis 8, God started over with
eight people: Noah and his wife, and their three sons and their
wives. In Genesis 8:17, God gave Noah the same mandate He
gave Adam and Eve: "be fruitful and multiply." If we're tempted to
think, "Finally! God got rid of all the bad apples with the flood,"
not so fast. In Genesis 8:21, after the flood, God repeated His
earlier pre-flood sentiment concerning sinful humanity by saying
"the intention of man's heart is evil from his youth."

Sadly, the sinful nature was here to stay, and we see it immediately in Noah getting drunk and his son uncovering his nakedness

(whatever that means, it's not good!). That's in Genesis 9. In Genesis 10, we see the genealogy of Noah and his sons, and in the last verse of chapter 10, it says something very interesting:

> *These are the clans of the sons of Noah, according to their genealogies, in their **nations** [same root word for ethnos in the LXX], and from these the **nations** [ethnos in the LXX] spread abroad on the earth after the flood. (Gen. 10:32)*

Here, as well as earlier in Genesis 10 (vv. 1, 5, 20, and 31), is where we first find the idea of ethnicity in the Bible. In verse 32, we learn that people began to spread throughout the world after the flood. The account of the Tower of Babel immediately follows and gives us the details of how this happened. Babel is a crucial turning point in Scripture, as it is the segue into the story of Abraham, who is a key figure in God's plan of redemption. But before we dive into the Tower of Babel and its implications, now is a good time to address the problem of how we usually talk about "racism."

The Problems with "Racism"

There are a number of problems with the term "racism." First, as I mentioned, "race" as we know it is not a biblical category. In saying that, I'm not saying that "racism" doesn't exist. I'm saying that we can be more biblical in how we discuss what we mean when we say "racism." The term "racism" is already loaded with unbiblical assumptions. I don't think Christians should surrender to the culture by embracing terms that are embedded with faulty frameworks. Second, the term "racism," as used in common parlance, is so broad that it can say too little and too much simultaneously. So for instance, many people, when they hear "racism," think Ku Klux Klan and Dylann Roof, the White nationalist who murdered nine Black church members at a Bible study in Charleston, South Carolina in 2015. That is, "racism" is conscious hatred toward another person or group because of their "race" that often leads to violence against them. For others, "racism" may include individual animosity, but actually goes much further than that. It can also manifest itself in systems and institutions that have detrimental effects on its victims even when there is no personal animosity on the part of the players involved. It could also refer to holding to stereotypes about groups of people or having negative preconceived notions (prejudice) about people based on their "race." It could refer to unconscious bias. Further, it may refer to discriminatory practices that exclude people of certain "races" from opportunities, wealth, or advancement in society. It could also refer to using disparaging language or terminology when referring to different "races."

These are just a small sampling of the myriad ways that "racism" is used. The problem should be apparent immediately. If I say that someone is guilty of "racism," where on this spectrum am I placing them? Are we ready to equate someone who has an unconscious bias toward a group of people with the KKK? Surely, a topic this serious deserves the benefit of layers and nuance! If we as Christians are going to address sin, especially in other believers, it's important that we address it specifically and with biblical categories. I think there's a better way. I want to list out six things that people may mean when they say "racism," while using language more in line with Scripture. In doing so, I'm simply combining the more biblical terminology of ethnicity with sins that are commonly alluded to in the Bible. In other words, these are particular sins that manifest themselves in the realm of ethnicity. I will include both modern and scriptural examples for each.

Common Ethnic Sins

Ethnic Hatred

Ethnic hatred is often what people mean when they talk about "racism." It may be the most obvious of the ethnic sins. This is an active, passionate disdain for another person or group based on their ethnicity. This contempt often leads to violence and murder. Modern examples of this are the Ku Klux Klan and neo-Nazis. Biblical examples of this would be Haman toward the Jews (Est. 9:24) and Jonah toward the Assyrians (Nineveh was the capital of Assyria). Jonah had so much contempt for them that he couldn't even find it in his heart to rejoice when Nineveh repented at his preaching (Jonah 4:1).[7]

Ethnic Pride

A subtler sin than ethnic hatred, ethnic pride is when a person has feelings of superiority concerning the ethnic group they belong to. This is often accompanied by viewing other ethnic groups as inferior. Modern examples of this are as blatant as the Black Hebrew Israelites or as subtle as a condescending comment made by an American homeowner to the immigrant worker who does her landscaping. Biblical examples of this would be Goliath concerning Israel (1 Sam. 17:8) and the Jews concerning Gentiles (Rom. 2:17–29).

Ethnic Favoritism (or Partiality)

Ethnic favoritism is the practice of giving unjust preferential treatment to one person or group on the basis of their ethnicity. A modern example of this is Wells Fargo Bank settling an $8 million lawsuit in 2020 from the US Department of Labor due to charges of discriminatory hiring practices that proved detrimental to thousands of Black applicants. As part of the settlement agreement, Wells Fargo admitted no liability, but also agreed to provide job opportunities to 580 of the impacted applicants.[8]

Whether liable or not, the charge was ethnic favoritism. In fact, Wells Fargo has paid out hundreds of millions of dollars to settle discrimination lawsuits over the years. This charge has also been levied against teams in the National Football League, who some believe regularly overlook qualified minority coaches in favor of White coaches. Additionally, when people take issue with programs like Affirmative Action, it's often because they believe companies and institutions that practice them are guilty of ethnic favoritism. I have two biblical examples. One is the explicit command against favoritism.

> *If, however, you show favoritism, you commit sin and are convicted by the law as transgressors. (James 2:9 CSB)*

In the context of James, the favoritism was on the basis of economic status, but obviously the command forbids favoritism on any basis, including ethnicity. The second example is in Galatians 2, when Peter chooses to eat with Jewish Christians rather than Gentile Christians. I'll address this more a little later.

Ethnic Oppression

Ethnic oppression is the unjust or cruel exercise of power or authority toward a person or people on the basis of their ethnicity. Modern examples of this are the displacement of Native Americans in the US and the mass incarceration of Black men in America during the "War on Drugs" in the '80s and '90s.[9] Biblical examples of this are the oppression of the Hebrews by the Egyptians (Ex. 3:9) and the oppression of Israel by the Midianites (Judg. 6:1–10).

Ethnic Idolatry

Ethnic idolatry is elevating one's own ethnicity (or someone else's) to a place that causes the person to break the law of God. A modern example is the Christian parents who forbid their Christian child to marry another Christian because of their ethnicity. The Bible is crystal clear that, as long as it's a lawful marriage, there are no ethnic restrictions whatsoever. The only consideration in that case is whether or not the other person is a Christian ("in the Lord" in 1 Cor. 7:39). Ethnic idolatry occurs whenever a Christian makes their ethnicity their primary and ultimate identity, rather than the fact that they are united to Christ.

Ethnic idolatry can also apply to other ethnicities, i.e., when one covets another person's ethnicity (Col. 3:5). One infamous modern example of that is Rachel Dolezal, the White woman who deceived many people into thinking she was Black, going so far as to become a chapter president of the NAACP.[10] Ethnic idolatry can also occur when a person's love for another ethnicity is so great that it causes them to hate themselves or people from their own ethnicity. Biblical examples of ethnic idolatry are Miriam and Aaron criticizing Moses for marrying a Cushite woman

(Num. 12:1–16) and Solomon with his foreign wives who led him to worship false gods (1 Kings 11:1–8).

Ethnic Neglect

Ethnic neglect is a sin of omission. It occurs when a person fails to care properly for another person because of their ethnicity. This is a violation of Proverbs 3:27: "Do not withhold good from those to whom it is due, when it is in your power to do it." A modern example would be the seventeen White police officers who stood there while Rodney King was being beaten and did nothing to intervene. Related to that case was the case of Reginald Denny, the White truck driver who was pulled out of his truck during the L.A. riots and viciously assaulted by a group of Black men. The other Black people who stood around and watched (or worse, laughed) were guilty of ethnic neglect. Thankfully for Denny, there were four other Black people who didn't give in to that temptation and came to his rescue.[11] A famous biblical example would be the priest and the Levite who were guilty of ethnic neglect in the parable of the Good Samaritan (Luke 10:30–37). A lesser-known example is how the disciples responded to the Canaanite woman in Matthew 15:23.

It should be plain to see that each of these sins is, at the root, a failure to love neighbor as self. They also cover a range wide enough to indict most of us. I suspect that the Christian who balks at the possibility of being a "racist" would look at this list and see temptations that have gripped their own hearts. And praise be to God that the blood of Jesus Christ is sufficient to cover these sins as well. I believe that this kind of specificity will serve us as we dialogue on these issues in the church.

Let's Talk Some Babel

The account of the Tower of Babel in Genesis 11 is one of the most famous stories in the Bible. In it, we learn that everyone at that time spoke the same language. In their pride, a group of people decided to build a tower that stretched all the way to the heavens. As they were building it, God struck them down, and in the process, confused their language, which caused them to scatter throughout the world. Seems pretty straightforward. But a closer reading of the passage reveals some important lessons about unity.

Sinful Humanity United Against God

Genesis 11:1

> Now the whole earth had one language and the same words.

In verse 1, we see both a statement of unity and the basis of that unity. There was one common language. This is exactly what natural unity looks like. There's some external characteristic that brings people together. In and of itself, it's not a bad thing. Speaking the same language is essential to effective communication. However, there is nothing supernatural about this kind of unity. It's *natural* unity. You don't need the Spirit of God to be united because you all speak the same language.

People unite around all kinds of things. Music is a big one. We've all either seen video or perhaps we've been to a packed arena filled with people united around their love for a certain artist. Sports is another one. I remember taking a trip to London a few years ago. It just so happens that I was there the same weekend that my hometown team, the Philadelphia Eagles (no jokes, please), was playing there. Thousands of fans had crossed the Atlantic on a pilgrimage to watch their team. (As fans, we're not as bad as our reputation. We're worse.) At the airport in Philly, I happened to have on my Eagles sweatshirt. As I walked through the concourse, an elderly White woman who looked to be in her seventies silently smiled and with great intensity and earnestness, she gave me the thumbs-up sign. In that moment two people who differed in age, ethnicity, and gender had a brief moment of unity.

When the Eagles won the Super Bowl in February 2018 and had the parade in Philly, one thing that people pointed out more than anything else is how diverse the crowd was. Young and old. Kids and parents. Rich and poor. Police and civilians. On that day, Black and White didn't matter. The only color that mattered was green—the Eagles' colors that flooded Broad Street that day. Everybody was happy. There was no violence or arrests, just celebration. For some of the Christians who were there, it was bittersweet. On the one hand, it's nice to see unity. On the other hand, we know that, ultimately, it was fleeting. But it did leave people wondering why it seems to be so rare that we see this kind of thing in the church, where the basis of our unity is much deeper than language or a sports team.

In Genesis 11, we see a group of people with natural unity. And we also see the outcome of natural unity when it's not accompanied by faith. Ultimately, it's a unity that is opposed to God.

God Thwarts Sinful Man's Plans

Genesis 11:6–7

And the LORD said, "Behold, they are one people, and they have all one language, and this is only the beginning of what they will do. And nothing that they propose to do will now be impossible for them. Come, let us go down and there confuse their language, so that they may not understand one another's speech."

When God looked at the people of Babel, He saw a unity that was in opposition to Him. He recognized the destructive power of this godless unity, and He swiftly dealt with it. Here we see God's sovereign power on display. He shows that He's active in this world. He's not an absentee God. He's aware of everything, and "it is the purpose of the LORD that will stand" (Prov. 19:21).

Can you imagine being on that construction site? Imagine the person you were just talking with seconds ago begins to speak, but all you hear is "Wah Wah Wah" like Charlie Brown's teacher! How long did it take before they realized the person was speaking another language? Did they have a meeting where only some people understood some and others understood others? How do you have a meeting when you can't communicate?

You see what God does? He takes away the basis of the natural unity when it's opposed to Him. This is why every fallen, earthly institution and group and society will eventually perish. Death has a way of doing that. Only one institution will survive judgment day and continue into the age to come—the church. The Lord Jesus said in Matthew 16:18,

"...I will build my church, and the gates of Hades will not overpower it." (CSB)

The point there is that Hades is the realm of death. All human institutions are eventually brought to an end when the people that created them die off. Not so with the church. Even though individual believers may die, God will preserve a people for His name's sake until He returns.

Any unity that is not of God will ultimately be thwarted by God. Unity that is of God will be blessed by God. This is why the church should be at the forefront of displaying what it means for diverse people to come together in the name of Christ and showing off the beauty of God by the way we love each other. Sadly, this has often not been the case, either historically or today. One of Satan's tricks is to take natural unity but dress it up in Christian disguise.

> Any unity that is not of God will ultimately be thwarted by God. Unity that is of God will be blessed by God.

One tragic historical example of this are those who united around the transatlantic slave trade, both the European slave traders and the African chiefs who sold their people. That was natural, sinful unity based on ethnic pride, ethnic hatred, and greed. That's the very definition of unity in opposition to God. Some even went so far as to seek religious justification for it with bad interpretations of biblical texts. This is how professing Christians participated in chattel slavery. Frederick Douglass recognized this and wrote about it in scathing terms:

Between the Christianity of this land and the Christianity of Christ, I recognize the widest possible difference—so wide that to receive the one as good, pure, and holy, is of necessity to reject the other as bad, corrupt, and wicked. To be the friend of the one is of necessity to be the enemy of the other. I love the pure, peaceable, and impartial Christianity of Christ; I therefore hate the corrupt, slave-holding, women-whipping, cradle-plundering, partial and hypocritical Christianity of this land. Indeed, I can see no reason but the most deceitful one for calling the religion of this land Christianity.[12]

As we saw earlier, the Southern Baptist Convention was formed by people who defended pastors and missionaries being slave owners. When you look into most of the older religious denominations you find similar compromises. This is what the fall has done. It takes that which should glorify God and turns it into an opportunity to divide, hate, marginalize, and oppress, even in the name of Christ.

But consider those who did this back then. Where are they now? The transatlantic slave trade? Where is it? It's gone, praise be to God! God thwarted that unity. But guess what is still here? That's right. The church.

It's no accident that immediately following the account of the Tower of Babel, in the very next chapter we get introduced to Abraham. Through Babel, God scattered people throughout the nations. But it wasn't to leave them there without hope and without God in the world. Through Abraham's seed, God had a plan to bring them back and unite all ethnic groups to demonstrate that what the people of Babel meant for evil, God meant for good.

Chapter 8

Father Abraham Had Many Sons

As an adult convert to Christianity, who didn't grow up in the church, I missed out on things like Vacation Bible School. So I was late to the party when it came to Christian jingles for kids. At the classical Christian school my children go to, they were recently taught the VBS classic "Father Abraham."[1]

The lyrics are simple and tell us that Abraham had "many sons," and we're among them. Praise the Lord! After the singing, hands and feet get involved. It's a blast. Even though the lyrics don't rhyme, the song is pretty catchy. But I do wonder how many unsuspecting five-year-olds come away completely confused: "*I'm* one of Abraham's sons? Mommy and Daddy told me that his sons were Ishmael and Isaac. Also, I'm a girl!" As simple as that song may be, the truth it is communicating is a theological gold mine. It's also relevant to our discussion on ethnicity.

Babel's Aftermath

At the end of our last chapter, we saw how God thwarted the unity of the people of Babel by confusing their language. In the next verses in Genesis 11, we see the results of God's judgment.

Genesis 11:8–9

> *So the LORD dispersed them from there over the face of all the earth and they left off building the city. Therefore its name was called Babel, because there the LORD confused the language of all the earth. And from there the LORD dispersed them over the face of all the earth.*

So here it is. We took a slight detour in Genesis 11, but now we see that the Tower of Babel story is the explanation of Genesis 10:32: how "the nations spread abroad on the earth after the flood."

The sovereign LORD used this instance of sinful people with sinful purposes to spread them out and repopulate the earth. At this point in time, it was primarily unbelievers. These are the people so often referred to as the nations, or the Gentiles. Immediately after Genesis 11 comes Genesis 12, where God begins the unfolding of His purposes with the calling of Abram. As we follow Abram's story, we see God making a covenant with him in Genesis 15. And in Genesis 17:5, God renames Abram:

*"No longer shall your name be called Abram, but your
name shall be Abraham, for I have made you the father of a
multitude of nations."*

From a human standpoint, this seems absurd because at the
time, Abram was ninety-nine years old and had not had any children with his wife yet. And yet God is giving him a name that
means "father of multitudes." It must have made people chuckle
under their breath when a man older than their grandparents told
them, "Don't call me Abram anymore. Call me Abraham." But as
we continue the story, we see that there was a reason God spread
people all over the earth and allowed them to develop their own
societies, tribes, and languages. God's purpose was that the nations
formed through the disobedience of Babel would ultimately be
united through the obedience of Christ.

In Genesis 12:1–3, we read about God's call on Abram and His
promise that He will make of him "a great nation," bless him, and
make his name great. Not only that but God told Abram: "I will
bless those who bless you, and him who dishonors you I will curse,
and in you all the families of the earth shall be blessed" (v. 3).

If we want to know how to properly understand this passage,
there's a great commentary on it that I want to highly recommend
to you. It's published by the Holy Spirit in a book called Galatians in the New Testament. Here's the inspired interpretation of
Genesis 12:3:

*Know then that it is those of faith who are the sons of
Abraham. And the Scripture, foreseeing that God would
justify the Gentiles by faith, preached the gospel beforehand to
Abraham, saying, "In you shall all the nations be blessed." So*

then, those who are of faith are blessed along with Abraham,
the man of faith. (Gal. 3:7–9)

Here we see a number of things. First, we see the answer to the
riddle, how can one man be the father of a multitude of nations?
The shocking answer that the apostle Paul gives is that through
faith in Jesus Christ, even Gentiles can be sons of Abraham! This
is because Christ was "slain, and by [His] blood [He] ransomed
people for God from every tribe and language and people and
nation [ethnos]" (Rev. 5:9).

Abraham's Gospel

The second thing we see here is Paul saying that God (He's person-
ifying Scripture here, but it was God speaking in the passage he's
quoting) preached the gospel to Abraham. Have you ever read a
passage in the Bible for many years and then discovered something
in a text that made you feel like you'd never read it before? That happened to me with this passage. In Genesis 12:3, God was preaching
the gospel . . . to *Abraham?* And what exactly was the content of this
gospel God preached? "In you shall all the nations (ethne—same
root word) be blessed." Embedded into Abraham's gospel was God's
plan for a global multiethnic church to receive the blessing of salvation through Christ! This is why ethnic diversity is so important.

"Whether Jew or Gentile"

This brings us to perhaps the biggest issue in the New Testament
concerning how God's people interacted with each other: the

Jewish/Gentile conflict. We see it alluded to in Acts 15, Romans 14, 1 Corinthians 8, and numerous other places. The entire book of Galatians is dealing with this issue. The conflict basically boiled down to this question: how were Jews supposed to rightly respond to Gentiles being included in the covenant people of God? For us in the twenty-first century, when the church is primarily Gentile, it's hard to appreciate the magnitude of this issue for first-century Jewish people.

For thousands of years after the calling of Abram, God had exclusively worked His saving power among the Jews, with a few Gentiles sprinkled in here and there. God made it abundantly clear to Israel that He had set them apart from all other peoples on the earth. In Deuteronomy 7, upon their deliverance from slavery in Egypt, the Lord discloses to Israel who they are, what He did for them, and why He did it:

> *"For you are a people holy to the LORD your God. The LORD your God has chosen you to be a people for his treasured possession, out of all the peoples who are on the face of the earth." (vv. 6–7)*

In the verses that follow, God makes it clear that it wasn't the greatness of Israel that prompted Him to choose them, but rather His love and His promise (vv. 7–8).

Through the prophet Amos, as God warns Israel concerning their rebellion and idolatry, He reminds them about their unique access to God:

> *"You only have I known*
> *of all the families of the earth." (Amos 3:2a)*

Notice how the Psalmist celebrates this fact in Psalm 147:19–20:

> *He declares his word to Jacob,*
> > *his statutes and rules to Israel.*
> *He has not dealt thus with any other nation;*
> > *they do not know his rules.*
> *Praise the* LORD*!*

The apostle Paul urges the Gentile converts in Ephesus to consider their dire situation before the coming of Christ:

> *Therefore remember that at one time you Gentiles in the flesh,*
> *called "the uncircumcision" by what is called the circumcision,*
> *which is made in the flesh by hands—remember that you*
> *were at that time separated from Christ, alienated from the*
> *commonwealth of Israel and strangers to the covenants of*
> *promise, having no hope and without God in the world.*
> *(Eph. 2:11–12)*

Before Jesus came, the only way for a Gentile to have a relationship with God was for them to religiously and culturally become a Jew. One result of God's selection of Israel is that, for thousands of years, Jews maintained a consistent, distinct culture derived from the law. By the time we get to the New Testament, a deep disdain for Gentiles had grown in the hearts of many Jews. And this was not only a religious issue. It was an ethnicity issue as well. In the mind of Jews, Gentiles were not only ceremonially unclean, but socially and culturally unclean as well. There was without question some ethnic superiority at work. But with the coming of Christ and the spread of the gospel beyond Jerusalem and Israel, what we begin to see is many Gentiles coming to faith. This brought up some crucial questions, such as: What about all the Old Testament civil and ceremonial laws? Did they apply to Gentiles? What about circumcision? Did Gentiles need to be circumcised? Many New Testament passages are dedicated to addressing these questions.

In this, we can see the wisdom of God. God knew that because of the fall, ethnic and cultural division would always be an issue for God's people in the world until Christ returns. So He leveraged this Jewish/Gentile conflict and inspired in Scripture the working out of strife and tension between Christians of different cultures and ethnicities. This was so that wherever the gospel spread until the return of Christ, the church would have tools for addressing these issues in ways that distinguished them from the surrounding culture. One example of this tension is the situation in Galatians 2:11–14, where Paul confronted Peter.

Peter had been eating with the Gentiles. In the historical context, eating together was a sign of deep fellowship. How do you get a first-century Jew and Gentile eating together? How is that possible? The gospel! Jesus broke down the dividing wall of hostility that stood between Jew and Gentile (Eph. 2:14). He made the two one. So in sharing deep fellowship with Gentiles, Peter was living out an implication of the gospel.

But then something happened. Verse 12 says that certain men came from James. These were people of the "circumcision party." These were the "militant" Jews. And Peter, perhaps out of fear of what they would say or do or think of him, decided to separate himself from the Gentiles. This is a clear case of ethnic favoritism. And he influenced the Son of Encouragement himself, Barnabas. This behavior received a sharp rebuke from Paul. Notice what he says in verse 14:

> *But when I saw that their conduct was **not in step with the truth of the gospel** . . .*

In Paul's mind, this was a gospel issue. Returning to the ethnic and cultural division of the past was a violation of the truth of the gospel. What does the gospel say? The gospel says that Jesus died for all people groups without distinction. Jesus made no ethnic distinctions in who He died for, so why would His people make ethnic distinctions in who they fellowship with?

> **Jesus made no ethnic distinctions in who He died for, so why would His people make ethnic distinctions in who they fellowship with?**

Peter knew this. God had revealed this to him in a vision on a rooftop in Acts 10:9–16. As Peter processed the vision, he came to the following conclusion that he shared with the Gentiles who were sent to him from Cornelius, a Roman centurion.

> *And he said to them, "You yourselves know how unlawful it is for a Jew to associate with or to visit anyone of another nation, but God has shown me that I should not call any person common or unclean." (Acts 10:28)*

When Peter met Cornelius the next day, he was bold enough to stand up in a crowded room of people and make a revolutionary statement on this landmark moment between Jew and Gentile in redemptive history:

So Peter opened his mouth and said: "Truly I understand that God shows no partiality, but in every nation anyone who fears him and does what is right is acceptable to him."
(Acts 10:34–35)

In Acts 15, when the Jerusalem council was convened on the question of whether Gentiles needed to be circumcised, Peter, this time in front of the other apostles and elders (v. 6), was very clear on this subject. Concerning Gentiles, Peter said that God "made no distinction between us and them, having cleansed their hearts by faith" (v. 9).

For Peter, disassociating himself from his Gentile brothers in Christ in Galatians 2 wasn't a matter of ignorance. He knew the truth. But, as we all know, old habits are hard to break. Whether it was fear of man or something else, Peter was allowing his old ethnic biases to prevent him from living out present gospel implications.

Does Ethnicity Matter?

Many well-meaning Christians believe that we should never talk about ethnicity. And I get it. It just seems too divisive. Why bring it up at all? And they'll often quote a verse that comes later in Galatians 3:28:

There is neither Jew nor Greek, there is neither slave nor free, there is no male and female, for you are all one in Christ Jesus.

In context, Paul is making a contrast between the old covenant law and God's new covenant promise. He's showing that the law was insufficient to save. For Jews, the law served as a "guardian until Christ came" (v. 24). But the promise is more glorious than the law, and through faith in Christ, the Gentiles are partakers of the promise.

Paul's point is that Gentiles are included among the people of God simply because they trust in Christ. To truly be a child of Abraham has a spiritual significance that surpasses earthly lineage. Verse 28 does not eliminate ethnic distinctions any more than it eliminates gender distinctions when it speaks of male and female. The point is that ethnicity, social, or economic status, and gender are not barriers to being justified before God through faith in Jesus. So to the question, does ethnicity matter? I respond with another question. Does it matter *for what*? For salvation? Absolutely not! But in order to display the glory and wisdom of God, it definitely matters that God made you Jamaican or Italian or Irish or Korean or Polish or Turkish or Taiwanese or Nigerian. Like everything else in the world, ethnicity exists for God's glory. I wrote a song for children about this called "God Made Me and You." On the second verse, I point them (and us) to the beauty of God's diversity in human beings:

> *Just as two snowflakes are never the same*
> *Every person is different, unique in their frame*
> *God made them all—each kind and each sort*
> *He made some people tall and some people short*
> *Dark skin, light skin, and all in between*
> *In each color and shade, His beauty is seen*
> *The Lord knows the number of hairs on your head*
> *Whether brown or black; whether blonde, gray or red*
> *What some call ethnicity and others call race*
> *We should celebrate as a gift of God's grace*

You're wonderfully made from your feet to your face
Yup, God made me and you![2]

No matter what our outward appearance may be, all human beings have the unique honor of being created in God's image (Gen. 1:27). This is the biblical basis for treating all human beings with the dignity and respect that image bearers deserve. This is why slavery in America was evil. This is why many Christians today fight for the rights of the unborn and the elderly. And this is why the pursuit of justice for the poor and marginalized in any society is in line with the heartbeat of God (Prov. 21:3; Zech. 7:9–10).

When it comes to ethnicity, the proper response for the Christian is not to ignore it. Or gloat about it. Or be ashamed of it. Or feel guilty about it. The proper response is to thank God for it and leverage it for the glory of God. To my White brothers and sisters in Christ, please don't tell me that you don't see color. I know what you mean. You're trying to communicate that you treat all people equally and that you judge people based on the content of their character rather than the color of their skin. That's great. We should all do that. But God was intentional when He gave me brown skin. He didn't give it to me that it might be ignored. He gave it to me that it would be appreciated and that He might be praised for His creative genius. So don't rob God of His praise by ignoring it!

Whatever ethnic or cultural flavor you have, bring it to the table and offer it in service to Jesus. For me, that has looked like doing Christ-centered hip-hop. For Latino American Christians, it may look like starting a Bible study in Spanish for the immigrants in your area who don't speak English. For Jewish Christians, it may look like hosting a Passover seder in your home and showing those who attend how the elements point to Christ. At our church, which is multiethnic, we have events where members celebrate and become educated about the cultures of other members. One of my favorites was Korean night, where some of our Korean-American members treated us to some authentic Korean barbecue and helped us understand some of the cultural nuances in the Korean film we watched. There is plenty of room for creativity here. Let us not allow the way the world has corrupted ethnicity (through the sins of either pride or hatred) to keep us from using it to glorify God.

From Babel to Pentecost

In the last chapter, we saw the account in Genesis 11 of God confusing the language of the people in order to disperse them among the nations. Many centuries later, in Jerusalem, fifty days after the resurrection of Christ, we learn in Acts 2:5 that there were Jews gathered there "from every nation under heaven" to celebrate the Feast of Weeks (Lev. 23:15–21). On this day, as the disciples were gathered in one place, the Holy Spirit arrived just as Jesus said He would. And when He came, as the old school Black preachers like to say, He "showed up and showed out." His arrival was accompanied by spectacular signs such as "a mighty rushing wind" and "tongues of fire" (Acts 2:2–3). But the greatest sign that day was that Jews from many different countries were able to hear each other speak in their own language.

Here we see the reversal of Babel. At Babel, we saw people united in opposition to God who were ultimately scattered by God. At Pentecost, we see people united in being chosen and gathered by God. They were supernaturally brought together by God, miraculously hearing each other in their native languages. And what were

134

they saying? They were "telling the mighty works of God" (v. 11). What mighty works of God? Without question, they were proclaiming the death and resurrection of Jesus Christ. I can't imagine a better use of language than that. The world is filled with many diverse kinds of people who are united in their opposition to God. May we as the church not be outdone by them or seek to mimic them. Rather, may we lead the way in displaying the unity of a diverse group of believers who have been reconciled to God, for the glory of God.

CHAPTER 9

Ethnicity and Justification

Brothers and sisters, we have a problem. There is ethnic disunity in the body of Christ, and that is a serious problem. If we take what the Bible has to say about division seriously, we'll recognize it as a serious problem. It doesn't take advanced observational skills to see the problem. It's obvious. I wrote this book to address that problem. Presumably, you're reading this book because you're concerned about that problem. If I were to ask you the question, "What is the key to addressing the problem of ethnic disunity in the church?" what would you say? I can imagine a range of answers.

Answer 1: The Humble Answer
"I don't know. That's why I'm reading the book!"
(Amen. God gives grace to the humble. Grace to you!)

Answer 2: The Oversimplified Answer
"The gospel."
(That's not necessarily wrong, but you're gonna need to unpack that a little bit.)

Answer 3: The Sunday School Answer
"Jesus."
(Can't go wrong with Jesus!)

Answer 4: The Self-Righteous Answer
"The key is those Christians over there getting it together and following the Bible (like we do)!"
(I bet you listen to sermons for other people, don't you?)

As you might expect from someone known for a style of music called lyrical theology, I'm going to suggest a theological answer. But it has nothing to do with music. It's because I firmly believe the best practices are deeply rooted in biblical principles. So what's my answer? The key to addressing ethnic disunity in the church is *the proper application of the doctrine of justification by faith alone.*

The Chief Article

As I mentioned in chapter 6, the doctrine of justification by faith alone is referred to by theologians as the material cause of the Reformation. Here's how the Westminster Shorter Catechism defines justification:

> *Justification is an act of God's free grace, wherein he pardoneth all our sins, and accepteth us as righteous in his*

sight, only for the righteousness of Christ imputed to us, and received by faith alone.[1]

To put it more simply, justification is God's declaration that a sinner is righteous through faith in Jesus Christ. That this is even possible is the greatest news that hell-bound rebels could ever hope to receive. There's a famous quote attributed to Martin Luther which says: "Justification is the article by which the church stands and falls."

Whether or not Luther actually said that, I don't know. But I do believe that the statement is true. There is a fuller quote that actually is from Luther that communicates the same sentiment, but more strongly:

> When the article of justification has fallen, everything has fallen. . . . This is the chief article from which all other doctrines have flowed. . . . It alone begets, nourishes, builds, preserves, and defends the church of God; and without it the church of God cannot exist for one hour. [It is] the master and prince, the lord and ruler, and the judge over all kinds of doctrines.[2]

What do you think when you read this? Is this hyperbole? Was Luther being overly dramatic? Was he exaggerating for effect? Can justification really be that important? When I reflect on the significance of this doctrine, my conclusion is that Luther had it right. Justification explains the mechanism at work behind how a person can be saved simply by trusting in Jesus. In Galatians 3:10, the apostle Paul addresses what is at stake for those who do not accept God's way of salvation, i.e., justification:

For all who rely on works of the law are under a curse; for it is written, "Cursed be everyone who does not abide by all things written in the Book of the Law, and do them."

In this fallen world, God has designed it so that there are only two ways that people can relate to God: law or grace. One condemns; the other saves. All human religion and false versions of Christianity involve some form of works-righteousness. In this passage, Paul reminds us that if we rely on our moral performance to make ourselves right with God, we are under a curse. The problem, of course, with trying to gain favor with God through obeying the law is that no one is able to do it. We judge ourselves by ourselves and foolishly assume that our standard is the same as God's. We'll all admit that nobody's perfect, as though that somehow lets us off the hook. But God requires *perfect* obedience. He refuses to lower His holy standard to accommodate sinful people. If we're going to pursue the fool's errand of salvation through the law, we can't be picky and choosy with what we obey. We must abide by *all* things written in the law. James 2:10 agrees with Galatians 3:10:

For whoever keeps the whole law but fails in one point has become guilty of all of it.

Many people think that as long as they're not breaking human laws, that means they're pretty good people. But while human laws may at times be based on God's law, God's standard is much higher. God's law not only governs outward actions, but inward attitudes. It not only deals with what we do, but what we think (Heb. 4:12) and what we say (Matt. 12:36). To illustrate how far short we fall, let's consider one of the Ten Commandments, which is a summary of God's law. Commandment number 10, which can be found in Exodus 20:17, says:

"You shall not covet your neighbor's house; you shall not covet your neighbor's wife, or his male servant, or his female servant, or his ox, or his donkey, or anything that is your neighbor's."

What does it mean to covet? Put simply, to covet is to have a strong desire. So the tenth commandment is forbidding us from having a strong desire for anything that belongs to someone else. We break this command anytime we have a strong desire for someone else's house, someone else's car, someone else's looks, someone else's property, someone else's gifts, someone else's popularity, someone else's money, someone else's grades, someone else's opportunities, someone else's athletic ability, someone else's status, someone else's wardrobe, someone else's job, someone else's ministry, someone else's personality, someone else's sense of humor, etc. I could go on, but you get the point.

The Westminster Shorter Catechism sums it up like this:

Q. 81. What is forbidden in the tenth commandment?
A. The tenth commandment forbiddeth all discontentment with our own estate, envying or grieving at the good of our neighbor.[3]

On the flip side,

Q. 80. What is required in the tenth commandment?

A. The tenth commandment requireth full contentment with our own condition, with a right and charitable frame of spirit toward our neighbor, and all that is his.[4]

Interestingly, in Colossians 3:5, it says that covetousness is idolatry, so whenever we break the tenth commandment, we're also breaking the first commandment, "you shall have no other gods before me." This means that a person can believe that the God of the Bible is the true God and that Jesus is the Son of God and still be an idolater in God's eyes because of a covetous heart. I think it's safe to say that the vast majority of people break this one command on a regular basis. There are entire industries like the advertising industry whose whole purpose is to stir up covetousness and discontentment. Please understand, we've only scratched the surface of that command, and there are nine more! I haven't even mentioned lying, stealing, dishonoring your parents, or taking the Lord's name in vain. But just consider this one command. If God were to judge you based on this one command alone, is there anyone who would feel confident standing before a holy God?

In light of that, in Galatians 3:11–12, Paul states what should be obvious to all who have properly considered the requirements of God's law:

> Now it is evident that no one is justified before God by the law, for "The righteous shall live by faith." But the law is not of faith, rather "The one who does them shall live by them."

Who would dare try to stand before a holy God on judgment day with their own personal law-keeping as the basis of their acceptance from God? Anyone who would feel comfortable with that scenario simply hasn't understood either the holiness of God (Deut. 4:24; Isa. 40:25; Hab. 1:13) or the depth of their sin (Ps. 51:5; Isa. 64:6; Jer. 17:9).

The Great Exchange

God's holiness exposes our sin for what it is. The law hangs over our heads like the blade of a guillotine, ready to drop at any moment and plunge us into eternal misery. There is no way for any sinner to escape the demands of the law. But praise be to God that He has provided another way!

> *Christ redeemed us from the curse of the law by becoming a curse for us—for it is written, "Cursed is everyone who is hanged on a tree"—so that in Christ Jesus the blessing of Abraham might come to the Gentiles, so that we might receive the promised Spirit through faith. (Gal. 3:13–14)*

The Lord Jesus Christ has done the unthinkable. He suffered the full curse of the law for all His people when He died on the cross. And according to the apostle, He did it so that every ethnic group might receive the Abrahamic blessing promised in Genesis 12:3. The flip side of this transaction is that Jesus perfectly obeyed God's law on behalf of His people, satisfying God's righteous demands in that regard as well. Paul mentions this in Romans 5:19, when he contrasts the work of Adam with the work of Christ:

> *For as by the one man's disobedience the many were made sinners, so by the one man's obedience the many will be made righteous.*

We mentioned earlier that God requires perfect obedience. There's only one person in the history of this world who was able to meet this demand: the Holy One of God, Jesus Christ. Through faith in Christ, believers receive credit not only for the death that Jesus died, but the sinless life that He lived! This transaction—our guilt for Christ's righteousness—is famously known as the Great Exchange.[5]

The glory of this truth cannot be overstated. This truth should have churchgoers shouting and dancing in the aisles! This truth should have us singing praises to God at the top of our lungs. This truth should cause us to resist sin with all of our might. This truth should compel us to lay down our lives for the gospel and for our brothers and sisters in Christ. This truth should prompt us to pursue ethnic unity in the church with all the strength that God supplies.

Justification and Ethnicity

Some may be reading this and thinking, "Amen. I agree that these things are true. But what does this have to do with ethnicity? My answer? It has *everything* to do with ethnicity! In Philippians 3:4–9, the apostle Paul speaks about the advantages he had before coming to Christ. What he came to realize is that the very things that he thought were spiritual assets were actually liabilities because they were keeping him from Christ. Nevertheless, from a human standpoint, his resume was pretty impressive. Check out what he says:

> *If anyone else thinks he has reason for confidence in the flesh,*
> *I have more: circumcised on the eighth day, of the people of*

Israel, of the tribe of Benjamin, a Hebrew of Hebrews; as to the law, a Pharisee; as to zeal, a persecutor of the church; as to righteousness under the law, blameless. But whatever gain I had, I counted as loss for the sake of Christ. Indeed, I count everything as loss because of the surpassing worth of knowing Christ Jesus my Lord. For his sake I have suffered the loss of all things and count them as rubbish, in order that I may gain Christ and be found in him, not having a righteousness of my own that comes from the law, but that which comes through faith in Christ, the righteousness from God that depends on faith.

Did you notice the advantages he mentioned? There are seven things on the list:

Circumcised on the eighth day—Religious advantage
Of the people of Israel—Ethnic advantage
Of the tribe of Benjamin—Ancestral advantage
A Hebrew of Hebrews—Cultural advantage
As to the law, a Pharisee—Educational advantage
As to zeal, a persecutor of the church—Personality advantage
As to righteousness under the law, blameless—Moral advantage

Out of the seven advantages mentioned, the first four certainly fall under the ethnicity umbrella, based on how we saw it defined in chapter 7. As impressive as those advantages may have been, however, none of them got him any closer to God. It's only when Paul was willing to reject his own righteousness and embrace the righteousness of Christ that he was saved. This is true for each one of us as well. There are a number of implications here:

The Doctrine of Justification Equips Us to Address Ethnic Sin in the Church

The very fact that we need to be justified assumes some things about us that are not flattering, to say the least. It assumes that we are guilty before God. It assumes that our sin against God deserves an eternal punishment. It assumes that there is nothing we can do to save ourselves. It assumes that, by nature, we regularly commit all kinds of evil in our thoughts, words and actions. Therefore, we can now recognize sin and call it what it is. We don't have to sugarcoat it or use euphemisms. We don't have to lie about the past, or do verbal gymnastics to avoid naming sin. Notice how the apostle Paul speaks when he addresses the church in Corinth:

> Or do you not know that the unrighteous will not inherit the kingdom of God? Do not be deceived: neither the sexually immoral, nor idolaters, nor adulterers, nor men who practice homosexuality, nor thieves, nor the greedy, nor drunkards, nor revilers, nor swindlers will inherit the kingdom of God. And such were some of you. But you were washed, you were sanctified, you were justified in the name of the Lord Jesus Christ and by the Spirit of our God. (1 Cor. 6:9–11)

Paul pulls no punches when it comes to naming the sins of the culture that characterized the Corinthians before they came to Christ. He's speaking very plainly. And before the believers with a tender conscience sink into despair or others allow their pride to deceive them into thinking they weren't that bad, what does Paul do? He reminds them that they were justified (v. 11). God set them apart and declared them to be righteous through faith in Christ. The gospel is big enough to cover the ethnic sins of Christians. When a Christian or a church truly embraces justification by faith alone in all its glorious practical ramifications, it will render defensiveness, rationalizing, and excuse-making obsolete.

The Doctrine of Justification Exhorts Us to Acknowledge Our Own Ethnic Sins

Maybe it's because of the confusion surrounding the term "racist," but many behave as if "racism" is the unforgivable sin in our culture. Hopefully the list of ethnic sins I listed earlier will help more of us to see ourselves and our own sinful tendencies in this regard. But it really baffles me that so many of us who embrace the doctrine of Total Depravity have such a hard time imagining that we might be guilty in this area. With a proper understanding of the doctrine of sin, we should actually find it surprising if most Christians *didn't* struggle with ethnic sins to some extent. For those of us who acknowledge that, justification by faith alone is really good news for us! As Pastor Tim Keller has stated:

> The gospel is this: We are more sinful and flawed in ourselves than we ever dared believe, yet at the very same time we are more loved and accepted in Jesus Christ than we ever dared hope.[6]

Justification by faith alone frees me up to admit my sinful tendencies toward ethnic pride and ethnic favoritism. The Holy Spirit gives me the power to turn from those things by God's grace. And the death of Christ on my behalf covers me when I fall short.

The Doctrine of Justification Empowers Us to Forgive the Ethnic Sins of Other Christians

In the same way that justification by faith applies to me, it also applies to my brothers and sisters in Christ. This means that I don't have to hold grudges against those who have confessed their own ethnic sins. I remember being in a small group book study at a predominantly White church I was a member of. At the time, we were studying the book *Bloodlines* by John Piper, which deals with Christians and ethnicity. There was a sweet White Christian lady who was committed to coming to the group. In fact, she was one of the few White Christians who showed up consistently. She had always been friendly toward Blair and me, and she seemed like the type of person who was willing to step out of her comfort zone in order to pursue understanding with different kinds of people.

> Something is wrong when God's Word is given to an ethnically mixed crowd and the sins of only one part of that crowd are addressed as though everyone else is guiltless.

One day, as I was walking home from the study, she called to me and caught up to me on the street. Her house was in the same direction as mine, so we walked together for a few blocks. As we walked, she said, "Shai, I have to confess something to you." "Okay," I said, not really knowing what to expect. She said, "Since I was young, I've really struggled with ... well ... I guess the only thing I can call it is racism." "Oh really?" I replied. I wasn't sure where this was going. She continued, "And it's not Black people in general. But it's specifically been toward Black men in particular. I've really struggled in this area, and I'm so sorry and I felt like I needed to ask your forgiveness." "I forgive you, sister," I said. It was one of the few times as a believer that I can remember a White Christian personally confessing to me that they were guilty of "racism." In the moment, it was an awkward conversation, but over time, I've really come to appreciate her willingness to humble herself in that way. Who was I to withhold forgiveness from someone that God has accepted through Christ?

The Doctrine of Justification Emboldens Us to Call Out the Ethnic Sins of Our Own Group

What justification by faith alone teaches us is that we're all sinful and guilty before God. No one ethnicity has cornered the market on sin. There's enough sin to go around for all of us. As a Black Christian, I can say that while historically in America Black people have been on the receiving end of much ethnic sin from White people, that doesn't mean we don't have our own sinful tendencies in this area. Ethnic pride, ethnic favoritism, ethnic hatred, and ethnic idolatry all have their manifestations in the Black community as well. But often, we get a free pass as we shine the spotlight squarely on White guilt. Something is wrong when God's Word is given to an ethnically mixed crowd and the sins of only one part of that crowd are addressed as though everyone else is guiltless. Justification by faith alone reminds us that even those who have historically been uniquely on the receiving end of sin are still sinners who also need a Savior.

The Doctrine of Justification Encourages Us to Find Our Ultimate Identity in Christ

Understood rightly, the doctrine of justification removes all notions (conscious or unconscious; spoken or unspoken) of ethnic superiority. We're taught that God's acceptance of us is not only without regard to the works we do, but without regard to our ethnic identity. In fact, justification teaches Christians that our primary identity is not our ethnicity, but our union with Jesus Christ. As I said in the last chapter, this isn't an argument for so-called color blindness. Rather, it's our primary identity in Christ that puts everything else about us that makes us unique in their proper place. This is Paul's point in Philippians 3:8:

> *Indeed, I count everything as loss because of the surpassing worth of knowing Christ Jesus my Lord. For his sake I have suffered the loss of all things and count them as rubbish, in order that I may gain Christ.*

This is what it's all about. Ethnicity has worth. It's valuable, beautiful, and reflects the wisdom and creativity of God. But compared to knowing Jesus, it's "loss" and "rubbish," along with anything else that would keep us from gaining the Lord. I love being Black. I'm thankful for how God made me. But God forbid I ever toss Jesus to the side for the sake of "Blackness." And God forbid I toss my White brothers and sisters in Christ to the side in some misguided attempt to prove my authentic Blackness. As Paul would say, that's rubbish. Jesus is so glorious that my aim is to be exactly who He's called me to be while at the same time being willing to let anything go that's not Him if it means getting more of Him. Because at the end of the day, He is what we all need. And He is more than enough.

OUR STORY

RY Part Four

Chapter 10

Jesus' Desire
for the Church

Anyone who has peered in on the "race" conversation in pockets of the American church in recent years must quickly conclude that Christians seem more divided than ever on this topic. With the amalgamation of religion and politics serving as a spark plug, the rhetoric on all sides of the debate has become increasingly hostile, malicious, and uncharitable. Some are convinced that the other side has bought into a left-wing liberal political agenda, making "race" a bigger deal than it is, seeing "racism" where it's nowhere to be found, and ignoring the progress that America has made since slavery, the Jim Crow era, and the Civil Rights Movement. Some are convinced that the other side has conflated Christianity with a right-wing conservative political agenda, denying obvious examples of "racism" and ignoring the present-day effects of over three hundred years of government-sanctioned oppression of Black people in the US. What makes the whole debate so perplexing is that both sides claim to follow the same Jesus, read the same Bible, and believe the same gospel.

In our arrogance, we assume that we're reading the Bible correctly and that those we disagree with are obviously in error. Chapter 22 in the gospel of Matthew is instructive for us in this regard. In this passage, there were two opposing religious groups, the Pharisees and the Sadducees, both of whom asked Jesus a series of questions to test Him. The Pharisees are considered by many to have been the theological conservatives of the day—the original "Bible Thumpers" with all their theological "i's" and "t's" meticulously dotted and crossed. The Sadducees are looked at by many as the theological liberals of the day—the original "Downgraders"—with a Jeffersonian penchant for splashing Wite-Out all over the supernatural passages in Scripture. As they questioned Jesus, the Lord displayed a biblical and rhetorical swordsmanship reminiscent of Obi-Wan Kenobi as He cut down the arguments of both groups one by one. By the end of the chapter, He managed to call them hypocrites (v. 18), inform them that they were wrong and didn't know the Scriptures or the power of God (v. 29), and stump them with a question about the Bible so hard that it left them speechless and unwilling to ever ask Him a question in public (v. 46), lest He make them look like fools in front of everyone again.

My point is not to say that there's a one-to-one correlation between Christians and those two religious groups. But there is enough in that account to cause us all to walk humbly before the Lord and one another. Both groups were religious. Both groups had followers. Both groups read the Scriptures. And both groups were dead wrong. My point is that when there are people who love Jesus and the Bible on the "other side" of the argument, we shouldn't automatically assume that we are the ones who are correct and in exact alignment with Jesus. In fact, we both might be wrong. Jesus had a way of indicting and offending everyone at some point in His ministry. Are we the special ones with whom Jesus just happens to agree at every point? Humility demands that we pray with David,

> When there are people who love Jesus and the Bible on the "other side" of the argument, we shouldn't automatically assume we are the ones who are correct and in alignment with Jesus.

> *Search me, O God, and know my heart!*
> *Try me and know my thoughts!*
> *And see if there be any grievous way in me,*
> *and lead me in the way everlasting! (Ps. 139:23–24)*

What Would Jesus Say?

Does Jesus have a word for us concerning the present divide over "race"? I believe He has something to say to Christians on all sides of the debate. What I have in mind is not something that He said to the disciples, but to His Father while He was praying. In John 17, the night before Jesus' death, after having His final discourse with the disciples and before heading to the cross, Jesus prayed what is known as the High Priestly Prayer. Here we get a chance to get a peek into Jesus' prayer closet and see what was on His mind as Calvary rapidly approached. He prayed concerning Himself (vv. 1–5) and His disciples (vv. 6–19). Beginning in verse 20, He shifts His focus from the disciples to "those who will believe in me through their word."

In this part of the prayer, Jesus, our Great High Priest, is interceding for Christians. And before we look at the specific things that Jesus desires for the church, I want to focus our attention on how Jesus identifies the church here. Those who "believe in Christ through their [the apostles'] word." What is the word of the apostles? Well, in verse 14, Jesus says that He gave the apostles the Father's word. So the Father gave the word to Jesus. Jesus gave it to the apostles (1 Cor. 15:3). Then it was preserved by those who came after the apostles and handed down to the church for her instruction until the end of the age when Jesus returns. That Word is the message of the gospel.

This is a good reminder that "faith comes from hearing, and hearing through the word of Christ" (Rom. 10:17). People become believers through the Word. Not through gimmicks. Not through marketing schemes. Not through politics. Not through activism. Not through man's wisdom, but the Word. If you are a Christian reading this, it's because you heard the message of the gospel and believed it. You heard that God is holy and must punish sin (Isa. 13:11). You heard that we have all sinned and gone astray (Isa. 53:6) and that our sin has separated us from God (Isa. 59:2). You heard that the day is coming when God is going to judge the world in righteousness (Ps. 96:13; Acts 17:31). You heard that this judgment includes the wrath of God for all eternity for all who stand before God without having their sins forgiven (Matt. 25:46).

You also heard that, in His love, God sent Jesus Christ into the world to save sinners (1 Tim. 1:15). You heard that Jesus lived a perfect life of obedience to God's law (Heb. 4:15). You heard that He died on the cross, paying the full price for the sins of all who would trust in Him (John 19:30). You heard that He rose from the grave on the third day (Matt. 28:6). You heard that the only way to be reconciled to God is through turning from your sins and trusting in the Savior (Mark 1:15). You did so, and you received the gift of eternal life (John 5:24). That's the word being referred to in John 17:20. This is the word of the cross from 1 Corinthians 1:18 that is "folly to those who are perishing, but to us who are being saved it is the power of God." It's that message that has saved you if you are a Christian reading this. And it's the message that can save you if you're not a Christian. With that said, let's take a look at John 17:20–23:

> *"I do not ask for these only, but also for those who will believe in me through their word, that they may all be one, just as you, Father, are in me, and I in you, that they also may be in us, so that the world may believe that you have sent me. The glory that you have given me I have given to them, that they may be one even as we are one, I in them and you in me, that they may become perfectly one, so that the world may know that you sent me and loved them even as you loved me."*

The Significance of Oneness

One of the things that is immediately striking about this passage is how often Jesus mentions oneness. Counting the times He uses the word "one" or the preposition "in," which indicates oneness, there are nine references in these four short verses. Clearly Jesus is concerned about oneness. When it says "one," that's an indication of unity. There are four observations I want to make about oneness from this passage that have implications for our pursuit of ethnic unity.

1. The oneness of the church is based on the oneness of God.

We see it in verse 21: ". . . that they may all be one, *just as* you, Father, are in me, and I in you." We also see it at the end of verse 22: ". . . that they may be one *even as* we are one."

Jesus is pointing back to the oneness (or unity) within God as the basis for the oneness (or unity) within the church. Here is where we must remember the doctrine of the Trinity. There is one God (1 Tim. 2:5). And within the one Being that is God, there eternally exists three co-equal, co-eternal Persons: Father, Son, and Holy Spirit (Matt. 28:19). The Bible clearly teaches that the Father is God, that Jesus is God, and that the Holy Spirit is God. They are distinct from one another. And yet, those three Persons are so united that it can truly be said that God is one. And that oneness is the basis for the oneness that Jesus speaks of concerning the church. This is why unity in the church is so important, because of what it says about God.

2. Christians are in spiritual union with Jesus Christ.

In verse 23 (see also v. 26), when Jesus says "I in them," He is alluding to what theologians refer to as the doctrine of the believer's union with Christ. Union with Christ is the teaching that by God's grace through faith, Christians are spiritually joined with Christ in such a way that all the salvation benefits that are inherently His become theirs by virtue of their covenantal relationship. This is a central theme throughout the New Testament, especially in the epistles written by the apostle Paul. It's so important and mysterious that it's referenced in many different ways. Rather than give a textbook definition, the Bible uses various kinds of illustrations to get the point across. We see it in John 15:5, where Jesus is the Vine and the church is the branches. We see it in numerous other places, such as 1 Corinthians 12:27, where the church is the body of Christ and Christ is the Head. We see it in Ephesians 5:32, where the church is the bride of Christ and Christ is the Husband. We see it in Ephesians 2:20, where the church is the temple of God, and Christ is the Cornerstone.

All of these images are pictures of our union with Christ. The Bible not only uses illustrations, but it describes each aspect of our salvation in these terms. Throughout the New Testament, Christians are referred to as:

Chosen *in* Christ (Eph. 1:4–5)

Made alive *in* Christ (Eph. 2:5)

New creations *in* Christ (2 Cor. 5:17)

Adopted *in* Christ (Gal. 3:26)

Crucified *with* Him (Gal. 2:20)

Buried *with* Him (Col. 2:12)

Seated *with* Him in the heavenly places (Eph. 2:6)

Justified *in* Christ (Rom. 8:1)

Sanctified *in* Christ (1 Cor. 1:2)

Glorified *with* Christ (Rom. 8:17)

We also see it in the ordinances of the church. Baptism is a visible picture of our union with Christ, when the Christian is baptized into Christ and His death (Rom. 6:3) and united with Him in His resurrection (Rom. 6:5). The Lord's Supper is a tangible experience that points to our union with Christ as we eat the bread, which represents Jesus' body, and drink the cup, which represents Jesus' blood.

This is why Ephesians 1:3 says: "Blessed be the God and Father of our Lord Jesus Christ, who has blessed us *in Christ* with every spiritual blessing in the heavenly places." Every blessing we receive comes as a result of our union with Jesus Christ.

Our union with Christ means that we have a spiritual communion with one another that transcends all natural earthly relationships. Division in the church is a denial of this profound reality.

3. The church is one.

In verse 21, Jesus prays "that they may all be one, just as you, Father, are in me, and I in you, that they also may be in us."

In verse 22, He prays: "The glory that you have given me I have given to them, that they may be one even as we are one."

These are prayers that will not go unanswered. If anyone gets His prayers answered, it's the Son of God, the Lord Jesus Christ! There's only one time that I know of that Jesus didn't receive what He asked for and that was in the garden of Gethsemane, when He asked for the cup of God's wrath to be removed from Him. And thanks be to God for that, because God's "no" to Jesus in that instance meant salvation for us. Jesus' prayers get answered. The oneness that Jesus was praying for was purchased at the cross. The church is united to Christ and united to one another across all generations.

This brings up a question: if the church is one, why are Christians called to pursue unity, like in Ephesians 4:3, if we already have it? The answer is that when we pursue unity, we are living out the oneness that is already ours in Christ. It's similar to Romans 6:8, where it says "Now if we have died with Christ," but three verses later in verse 11 says, "So you also must consider yourselves dead to sin and alive to God in Christ Jesus." Well, which is it? Did we die with Christ? Or are we to consider ourselves dead? The answer is yes. He's saying you're dead. That's an objective fact of reality. Now, in light of that death, walk it out practically. It's the same idea with oneness. Christians are spiritually united through the work of Christ in the gospel. Now, we are called to walk in that oneness practically. We eagerly pursue it here knowing that it will ultimately be perfected in eternity.

4. Oneness has an evangelistic aim.

In verse 21, Jesus prays "that they may all be one, just as you, Father, are in me, and I in you, that they also may be in us."
Why?

> "So that the world may believe that you have sent me."

We see it again in verse 23:

> "I in them and you in me, that they may become perfectly one."

For what purpose?

> "So that the world may know that you sent me and loved them even as you loved me."

What we see here is that the oneness of the church is meant to be seen, not hidden. The Lord is teaching that when the church is walking in the unity that was purchased for us at the cross, it has a direct impact on our witness to a watching world. The unity of the church is one of the means that God uses to convince unbelievers that the God of the Bible is real.

> The unity of the church is one of the means that God uses to convince unbelievers that the God of the Bible is real.

One of my favorite parts of traveling to speak and do concerts is the fellowship with the saints after different events. I can't recall how many times I've been in restaurants after ministry events with large crowds of believers from different backgrounds at the table. Invariably, the server, with a look of bewilderment, will ask, "What is it that brings *you all* together?" For whatever reason, it's not registering in their minds how these people who look so different, who come from different age groups with different accents and styles of dress, could all be breaking bread at the same table and enjoying each other's company in such a familiar way. I've seen a number of gospel conversations started in just this way, with restaurant workers curious to learn more about a church that produces groups like this.

If the unity of the church is one of the means that God uses to convince unbelievers that God is real, sadly, the opposite is true as well. A divided church casts doubt or confirms doubts about the validity of the Christian's God and message. This is why God takes division among His people so seriously. We see that in these verses:

> *As for a person who stirs up division, after warning him*
> *once and then twice, have nothing more to do with him.*
> *(Titus 3:10)*

> *I appeal to you, brothers, by the name of our Lord Jesus*
> *Christ, that all of you agree, and that there be no divisions*
> *among you, but that you be united in the same mind and the*
> *same judgment. (1 Cor. 1:10)*

Division in the church communicates something false about God and His power to reconcile. When we look at how the church engages the issue of ethnicity in our informal gatherings, our Sunday school classes, our small groups, and on social media, what do we see? How would Jesus respond to the way we interact with Christians that we disagree with?

How to Walk in Unity

We see in John 17 that the unity of the church is important to Jesus. So how do we walk in unity when ethnicity seems to be such a divisive subject? We get some instruction from God's Word on this in Ephesians 4:1–6:

> *I therefore, a prisoner for the Lord, urge you to walk in*
> *a manner worthy of the calling to which you have been*
> *called, with all humility and gentleness, with patience, bearing*
> *with one another in love, eager to maintain the unity of*
> *the Spirit in the bond of peace. There is one body and one*

Spirit—just as you were called to the one hope that belongs to your call—one Lord, one faith, one baptism, one God and Father of all, who is over all and through all and in all.

In verses 4–6, we notice that, guided by the same Spirit, the apostle's teaching lines up exactly with what we saw in John 17. He grounds the unity of the church in seven objective realities:

One body
One Spirit
One hope
One Lord
One faith
One baptism
One God and Father

Paul's point is that the church in Ephesus is one. God, by His grace, has made them one. They have trusted the one triune God. They were baptized into one body. And this is all according to the one faith that was once for all delivered to the saints (Jude 3). Paul is saying, this is what you are, church. Now walk in it. And if you want to know what that looks like, the answer is in Ephesians 4:2: "with all humility and gentleness, with patience, bearing with one another in love."

That's what the pursuit of unity looks like for the Christian. There are many conversations surrounding ethnicity in the church today. I see a lot of anger. I see a lot of sarcasm. I see a lot of unforgiveness and mockery. What I don't see is a lot of humility, gentleness, patience, and bearing with one another in love.

Humility

Humility is seeing ourselves rightly before God. In the ethnicity discussion, it means actually listening to those who disagree with us, instead of just waiting to talk so we can get our points in. Humility asks, "Is there anything I can learn from this brother or sister?" Humility is being willing to admit that what we learned growing up (even in church) was actually wrong. Humility is a willingness to freely acknowledge the wrongs of those who belong to our own ethnic group. Humility is an openness to correction when we miss the mark. We would go a long way in the pursuit of ethnic unity if we as a church walked in humility toward each other.

Gentleness

Gentleness is related to the word often translated "meekness," which is strength under control. It is the disposition of a heart submitted to God. In the ethnicity discussion, it means refusing to lash out in anger toward believers who don't share our point of view. Gentleness governs how we speak, knowing that "a soft answer turns away wrath, but a harsh word stirs up anger" (Prov. 15:1). Gentleness is restrained, rather than explosive. Gentleness resists the temptation to "vent," but instead chooses to ask, "Can we pray?" Gentleness is unwilling to sacrifice a relationship for the sake of winning an argument. We would go a long way in the pursuit of ethnic unity if we as a church walked in gentleness toward each other.

Patience

The word translated "patience" literally means "to be long-tempered" as opposed to short-tempered. This is why it's translated in the King James Version as "longsuffering." It implies slowness to anger, even in the face of opposition. In the ethnicity discussion, it means not being easily offended by brothers or sisters who speak out of ignorance on the subject. Patience understands that it takes time for people to grow and is therefore willing to endure the dusty seed in hopes of one day seeing the flower in full bloom. Patience will sit down for hours to discuss and work through an issue, even if it doesn't change the other person's view, because patience is content with greater understanding being achieved by two siblings in Christ. Patience resists the urge to be outraged by every misstep or error other Christians make when dealing with ethnicity. We would go a long way in the pursuit of ethnic unity if we as a church walked in patience with each other.

Bearing with One Another in Love

Bearing with one another in love means avoiding resentment and bitterness toward our brothers and sisters in Christ with whom we disagree. It's resisting the impulse to retaliate or punish those who have hurt us. In the ethnicity discussion, it means moving toward, rather than away from, fellow church members who just don't seem to get it when it comes to ethnicity. Bearing with one another in love means not automatically "cancelling" a Christian who says something foolish, unhelpful, or even sinful regarding ethnicity. Bearing with one another in love means having open arms, ready to extend forgiveness when a believer says something insensitive or hurtful regarding ethnicity. Bearing with one another in love means pressing through the layers of misunderstanding, trusting that God is at work to sanctify both you and the Christian you disagree with. We would go a long way in the pursuit of ethnic unity if we as a church were serious and intentional about bearing with one another in love.

I Can Only Imagine

Imagine what our churches would be like if pastors modeled humility and gentleness when discussing ethnicity. How much progress would be made toward unity if congregations were patient with their pastors in this area? What if Christian social media personalities were known more for their gentleness than their sarcasm? How much ground would be gained in foreign missions if missionary agencies and missionaries on the front lines were characterized by humility toward the cultures of the ethnic groups they're trying to reach with the gospel? What if churches refused to split over nonessential differences because they were committed to bearing with one another in love? Imagine if seminary staffs, professors, and presidents took a posture of humility regarding the ethnic sins of its founders, treating the students who struggle with that with the utmost gentleness and patience?

What would this world be like if these things were so? My premillennial readers will read that and say, "It sounds like Christ has begun His millennial reign!" The rest of us will say it sounds like the new heavens and new earth. All jokes aside, brothers and sisters, we can be sure that this is the very thing that Jesus desires for His church. Careful readers may have noticed as you read the characteristics from Ephesians 4:2 that each one of those virtues are attributed to God elsewhere in Scripture. So in essence, these verses are anticipating Paul's exhortation a chapter later for Christians to be imitators of God (Eph. 5:1).

Concerning these commands, there's good news and bad news. The bad news is that all of us fall short on each of these things and that none of us can obey them in our own strength. The good news is that God has forgiven us for our failure in this regard and covered us with the righteousness of Christ, who perfectly modeled what it looks like to live an entire lifetime characterized by perfect humility, gentleness, patience, and forbearance. And by His Spirit, He empowers Christians to live out, albeit imperfectly, these virtues as we seek to walk in ethnic unity together. May it be so, for the glory of God.

Chapter 11

Agree in the Lord

In the summer of 2014, I was an elder at an SBC church in Northern Virginia. At the time, I was the only Black elder on the pastoral team, and my family was the only Black family in a predominantly White church. I was on staff there for two years as I prepared to plant a church back in Philadelphia. I had begun to preach through Philippians, which providentially coincided with a wave of video-recorded killings of unarmed Black people by police officers.

I was studying and preparing to preach the series when NYPD officers tried to arrest a 44-year-old Black man named Eric Garner, who was suspected of selling loose cigarettes that were untaxed. When officers attempted to handcuff Garner, he resisted, at which point he was taken to the ground. As numerous officers restrained him, Garner repeated the words "I can't breathe" a number of times. One White officer held Garner in a chokehold that had been previously banned by the NYPD. A Black female sergeant was among those who stood by and watched the incident unfold. Garner lost consciousness. He was pronounced dead about an hour later. The officers involved were not indicted. Garner's family eventually settled a wrongful death lawsuit with New York City for $5.9 million.

While I was preaching through Philippians 1, a 22-year-old Black man named John Crawford III was walking around in a Walmart in Beavercreek, Ohio, talking on a cellphone while holding a BB gun that he evidently intended to purchase. Responding to a 911 call about a man waving a gun, two White police officers arrived at the Walmart. According to the statements made by the officers involved, one of them opened fire after Crawford failed to comply with their orders to drop the gun. Crawford later died from his injuries at a nearby hospital. Surveillance video showed that he had not been waving the gun, and the person who originally made the 911 call admitted as much. After an investigation by the US Department of Justice, the officers were cleared of wrongdoing in the case. Crawford's family eventually settled a wrongful death lawsuit with the City of Beavercreek for $1.7 million.[1]

The day before I preached on Philippians 2, an 18-year-old Black man named Michael Brown Jr. was shot and killed by a White police officer in Ferguson, Missouri. The same evening that I preached the Philippians 2 sermon, my wife and I watched the news in disbelief as the riots began in Ferguson. This sparked months of unrest, protests, and arrests in Ferguson and around the country.

While I was preaching through Philippians 3, a 12-year-old Black boy in Cleveland, Ohio, named Tamir Rice was playing in a park when someone called 911 and reported that there was a person waving a gun. Unbeknownst to the officers who received the dispatch, the 911 caller said that the person with the gun was "probably a juvenile," and that the gun was "probably fake." Surveillance cameras showed two White officers swiftly approaching Tamir in their patrol car, and before the car could come to a complete stop, opening fire on Tamir and shooting him. Tamir died from his injuries the next day. No charges were ever filed in the case. Tamir's family eventually settled a wrongful death lawsuit with the City of Cleveland for $6 million.

On the Monday before I preached on Philippians 4:2–3, a grand jury declined to return an indictment for the officer involved in Michael Brown's death, meaning that he would not face criminal charges. This decision was followed by protests that eventually became violent, with some people setting cars and buildings on fire. The protests continued in different cities during the week as I was preparing to preach on that passage. Needless to say, I was distracted. Here I was, a Black pastor, called to help shepherd a predominantly White congregation. I was deeply grieved over what I was seeing in the media. But in my church, everyone seemed to be carrying on with life as usual as I mourned in silence. The other pastors were compassionate men who loved Jesus and loved me, but they couldn't relate to what I was feeling at the time. Perhaps there are readers who can't understand why I felt what I did. Many years later, I still can't adequately put it into words, but I'll make an attempt.

First, there's the shock of watching an image bearer die before your eyes on video. What hits me hardest is the finality of it all. One moment, they're alive. Sometimes, they're struggling in their last few seconds in this world, fighting to stay alive with all the energy they can muster. But by the time you get to the end of the video, they're gone. The solemn stillness of death has overtaken them. There's no coming back from it. Their fate is sealed and their destiny is fixed for all eternity.

Second, there's the violent nature of their deaths. Maybe it's my constitution. It would probably be a little unnerving for me to watch a video of someone dying peacefully in their sleep. But watching someone's life be extinguished via chokehold, strangulation, blunt force trauma, or gunshots is something I don't think anybody should become accustomed to. Yet, our culture somehow finds it normal for violent homicides to loop over and over on auto-playback on a computer screen adjacent to ads for skin cream and Doritos.

Third, there's the fact that I can often relate to the people who were killed because they look like people I know. Sometimes, they actually resemble our uncles, cousins, sons, coaches, and neighbors. Some of the people who were killed were engaged in criminal activity at the time they were killed by police. I certainly don't condone that. And I'm not even saying that the police were always unjustified in their use of force. Every case is different, and should be examined individually by each local jurisdiction to determine culpability. My point is that it's difficult for me to distinguish the people killed in those videos from the people I run into all the time at the corner store, the barbershop, cookouts, or family reunions. It takes very little imagination for me to put myself in the shoes of some of those who died.

Fourth, there's the real-life effects of these incidents. They disrupt your life in ways not anticipated. Perhaps it's due to the fact that some of the people killed were doing very normal things when they had the police called on them. In the years following the killings, there have been a number of incidents caught on video where White people have called the police on Black people for doing things like swimming in a public pool, working out in a private gym, sitting in a coffee shop, having a barbecue in a public park, and sleeping in a college dormitory.

In the wake of the Tamir Rice tragedy, my wife, Blair, and I were invited to the home of one of the elders for a get-together. At the time, we had two children. The kids were downstairs playing with the children of the other elders. At some point, Blair went downstairs to check on the kids and the boys were playing "cops and robbers" with toy guns. When my wife saw this, her heart sank. Immediately, she reflexively removed the toy from my son's hand, saying, "We don't play with these, son." Under other circumstances, maybe it wouldn't have been a big deal. What's more normal than four-year-old boys role-playing with toys? But when a Black boy just got killed by the police while playing with a toy gun, you view something that would otherwise be normal with different lenses.

Finally, there's the phenomenon that I can only refer to as the Collective Groan. This may be hard for some readers to understand, particularly if you're used to viewing things from a more individualistic standpoint. I, along with many other Black people in America, don't view these killings as isolated incidents in a vacuum, but as tragedies that have occurred within the context of our historical narrative as a people. The horrors of slavery; the lynchings of the Jim Crow era; the weaponization of firehoses and dogs in the Civil Rights Movement; the injustice of redlining; the murders of Emmitt Till, Medgar Evers, and Martin Luther King Jr.; the bombing of a church in Birmingham, killing four Black girls; the mass murder of Black church members at a Bible study in

Charleston; national headlines, seared into the African American psyche like a scorching hot branding iron seared into the flesh of a slave, combined with all of the daily humiliations, indignities, and brutalities that don't make the news, from the blatant discrimination that our grandparents told us about, to the glass ceilings that drove our fathers and uncles to despair; "the talk" about interacting with the police that's become a rite of passage in so many Black homes, and the myriad other ways that existence in America for so many Black people for so long has equated to a lifelong struggle to be viewed as fully human—all of these things contribute to the Collective Groan that causes so many Black people who see a White police officer kill an unarmed Black person to say, "Here we go again."

I had friends in the congregation, but as a pastor, I had to be guarded with what I shared with them about how I was feeling. On top of that, it seemed like people were withdrawing from me, perhaps out of fear of saying the wrong thing. So they said nothing at all, which in some ways was more painful. My wife was always ready to be a listening ear and a shoulder to cry on, but she admitted that while there's certain things she understood, she also knew that her experience as a Black woman was different than what a Black man goes through. The loneliness that I felt in those months was palpable and surreal. It all felt like it was reaching its nadir the very week I had to preach. As I studied the passage, I was blown away. At the very moment that I was at the height of my frustration with so many of my White brothers and sisters who seemed oblivious to the pain of so many people in the Black community, God, in His goodness, wisdom and sovereignty, had decreed that I would preach a sermon on unity in the church.

Sisters at War

In Philippians 4:2–3, we have a situation where two women in the church at Philippi are engaged in some kind of disagreement. In the midst of his letter to the church as a whole, the apostle Paul addresses these women directly:

I entreat Euodia and I entreat Syntyche to agree in the Lord. Yes, I ask you also, true companion, help these women, who have labored side by side with me in the gospel together with Clement and the rest of my fellow workers, whose names are in the book of life.

What can we as the church learn about ethnic unity from this passage? A few observations about the situation:

1. It was serious.

We don't know the specifics, but whatever the situation was, it was serious. And we know this because the women are mentioned by name: Euodia and Syntyche. This is one of the few times in his letters that Paul actually names names when addressing a conflict. Whatever was going on between these two women, it had made its way all the way from Philippi to Rome, where Paul was in jail. Their conflict was known in the church. And that makes sense. When two people openly disagree with each other, that kind of news tends to spread very quickly. We also know that it was serious because Paul requests help from a mediator in verse 3. "Yes, I ask you also, true companion, help these women." The words translated "true companion" indicate that Paul is addressing a specific person because the "you" in verse 3 is singular. You know the problem is serious when the two people involved can't resolve it themselves, and they need the help of an outside party to work through their differences.

2. Being Christians did not prevent them from having conflict.

It's clear that these women are Christians. We see that their names are "in the book of life" at the end of verse 3. And Paul tells them to agree "in the Lord" in verse 1. So these are believers we're talking about. They believe the same gospel. They serve the same Lord. They worship the same God. And yet they still have conflict. Knowing this should keep us from automatically excluding believers that disagree with us from the faith. This is especially dangerous when it comes to politics and voting. Historically in America, and generally speaking, Black Christians and White Christians have voted differently in presidential elections. There's a temptation to think, "How can they be Christians if they vote for _____?" In fact, some Christian leaders have gone so far as to publicly say things like, "If you're a true Christian, you'll vote for _____."

The problem with this is that whatever political party or candidate you endorse, you're going to be saying that an entire community of believers who vote differently isn't actually saved. Not only is this kind of thinking reductionistic and uncharitable, it's a distortion of the gospel of justification by faith alone. True Christianity is not determined by whether or not a person votes Democrat or Republican. It's determined by whether or not a person has placed their trust in the finished work of Jesus Christ on the cross, period. If we've learned anything from Jesus with the Pharisees, Paul with the Judaizers, and the Reformers with Rome, it's that we must not add to the gospel in this way. Euodia and Syntyche had a sharp disagreement. Presumably, one was right and the other was wrong. Or perhaps they were both wrong. But one or both of them being wrong did not exclude them from the kingdom of God.

3. Doing ministry together did not prevent them from having conflict.

We may be tempted to think, "If they're having trouble agreeing, these must have been immature Christians. Surely they were babes in Christ." That doesn't seem to be the case. These women were actually prominent in the church. Paul said that they "labored side by side with me in the gospel" (v. 3). (As an aside, I love how Paul affirms these women. He doesn't minimize their work. He doesn't place himself above them. In fact, affirming them would have been very countercultural in that society.) These women were in ministry with the apostle Paul! Can you imagine the conversation in heaven? Everyone is sitting in a circle reminiscing about life on the old earth. "What kind of ministry did you do in the old world?" "I did campus ministry." "I did some street evangelism". "I did Christian hip-hop." "Sister Euo? How about you?" "Oh, not much, I just labored side by side *with the apostle Paul.*" Euodia and Syntyche were working with the apostle day in and day out. They received his teaching, observed his example, and participated in his ministry. And yet, it's not all roses. These sisters were beefing with each other!

Why is that? The short answer is because of sin. Being a Christian doesn't exempt you from the conflict that comes from sin. Being in ministry doesn't exempt you either. In fact, the closer the relationship, the more likely you'll see conflict. Anyone who has ever been married, grew up with siblings, or had a roommate can testify to that.

I know this happened two thousand years ago, but it's just as true now as it was then. Don't let the Greek names fool you. If Paul had been writing this today, he could have just as easily said Michelle and Tiffany, or Patrice and Kellie, or Diane and Keisha—agree in the Lord!

It's really interesting what Paul *doesn't* say to them. He doesn't say, "Hey, Euodia, why did you do that to Syntyche?" Or "Syntyche, why did you say that to Euodia?" He doesn't refer to the actual issue at all. He simply addresses them both, begging them to agree. That phrase translated "agree in the Lord" uses the same words found in Philippians 2:2, "being of the same mind," as well as in Philippians 2:5, "Have this mind among yourselves," followed by Paul presenting the gospel in verses 6–11. What we're seeing in Philippians 4:2–3 is really just Philippians 2:1–5 fleshed out in a particular situation in the church.

Paul is going after the hearts of these women. I guarantee you that no matter what the issue was between them, if they both had the mindset of affection and sympathy, being of the same mind, and in humility counting the other as more significant than themselves, the issue would have been resolved immediately. If you look at the letter in this light, you get the sense that this is what Paul has been building up to all along. He speaks generally in Philippians 2:1–5 and specifically here. He is exhorting these sisters toward a heart posture that demonstrates a cross-centered perspective. Put another way, Paul is telling these women to *apply the gospel*!

Therefore, wherever you may land in the current debate over "race," I have an exhortation for you. My exhortation is what I believe God was saying to Euodia and Syntyche. It's what I believe

He was saying to Jew and Gentile. And what I believe He would say to Christians of all ethnicities today:

Labor to Develop a Spirit-Cultivated Affection and Sympathy for the "Other"

Each word and phrase in this sentence is meaningful. Let's look at them one by one.

Labor

We must labor because it's not something that just naturally happens. We tend to gravitate toward those we perceive to be most like us, whether that be ethnically, politically, or theologically. It takes intentionality and effort to move in love toward people outside our natural spheres.

Spirit-cultivated

Spirit-cultivated is meaningful because we can't perform this task in our own strength. Genuine affection and sympathy for people we don't connect with on some level must be wrought by the Spirit of God. If there's any kind of debate, battle, or contest between two people with the winner being decided by a vote, determining a winner is generally predictable by answering a simple question: who do the voters most identify with? When we identify with someone, we don't have to work as hard to develop affection and sympathy for them. But to do that for those we are naturally inclined to disregard, ignore, or even despise, that must come from the Holy Spirit.

Affection and Sympathy

I chose these two words in particular because they are found in Philippians 2:1:

So if there is any encouragement in Christ, any comfort from love, any participation in the Spirit, any affection and sympathy.

Let's look at those last two words:

Affection

Affection is important because it serves as fuel that can help us to continually lean into relationships, even when it's hard. Paul clearly had affection for the church at Philippi. Notice how he talks about them in Philippians 4:1:

Therefore, my brothers, whom I love and long for, my joy and crown, stand firm thus in the Lord, my beloved.

He could have simply said "stand firm in the Lord," but he's pouring it on thick because of his affection for them. This is after he already told them in chapter 1 that he holds them in his heart (v. 7) and yearns for them with the affection of Christ Jesus (v. 8). There is nothing distant or aloof about Paul's feelings toward these believers. His love and care for them are evident. Where is this affection between Christians who differ on the topic of ethnicity? Is it not the case that we're more likely to see pejorative labels, name calling, and distortions of the viewpoints of those with whom we disagree? It's far easier to dismiss someone as a "racist" than it is to love them enough to consider their genuine concerns. It takes far less effort to write someone off as a Marxist than it does to pray from the heart that God would comfort them in their grief, even if we can't understand it. May we, as the church, be so filled with the Spirit that onlookers would be able to discern the mutual affection we have for each other, even when we disagree.

Sympathy

Sympathy is meaningful because mutual understanding is impossible without it. The word translated "sympathy" in Philippians 2:1 is only used five times in the New Testament. Two of those times (Rom. 12:1; 2 Cor. 1:3) it's referring to God Himself. I'm a firm believer that sympathy is one of the primary keys to ethnic unity in the American church. This is so because part of the reason for the divide between Black and White Christians in America is a lack of shared experience. Due to historical factors, geography, and social stratification, it's possible for many White people in America to go their entire lives without having much meaningful interaction, let alone in-depth relationships, with Black people. Generally speaking, this is not as much the case for most Black people, as it's more common for us to encounter White people as teachers and counselors in our schools, coaches and teammates in youth sports, classmates and professors in college, and employers and coworkers on our jobs.

Part of the reason for the divide between Black and White Christians in America is a lack of shared experience.

Many White people have to make intentional decisions in order to have cross-cultural interactions. And often, when they do, it's on their terms. For example, it's far more common for Black Christians to join predominantly White churches than it is for White Christians to join predominantly Black churches. There are numerous sociological factors behind why many Black and White Christians see the world differently.[2]

We can bridge this divide when we proactively seek to sympathize with one another.

One example of this in my life happened around the time of the Ferguson protests. As I mentioned, I was having a hard time articulating all that I was feeling at that time. One of the other elders on the board was a White brother named Ben. Ben is one of the most encouraging brothers I've known as a believer. We are commanded to encourage one another in the Bible, but some people have the *gift of encouragement*. You know those rare people who thoughtfully and without resorting to flattery, have a way of speaking to you that leaves you feeling built up almost every time you're in their presence? That's Ben. Apart from the gospel, Ben and I didn't have much in common. We both grew up in Pennsylvania, but Ben grew up in an area that didn't have many Black people. And though we never really talked politics, my sense is that we probably landed in different places on certain political issues. Ben and I connected on love for God's Word and a desire to faithfully shepherd His people.

After church one Sunday, Ben approached me and asked me if he could treat me to lunch that week. When we sat down to eat, Ben said, "Shai, thanks for meeting me for lunch. The reason I asked you to lunch is that I wanted to know . . . if you wouldn't mind . . . could you please share with me what life has been like for you growing up as a Black man in America?" I was taken aback, because I had never been asked that question in that way from someone who was genuinely interested in hearing what I had to say.

For the next hour, Ben did nothing but listen as I poured out my heart. In my walk as a Christian, I can't remember many other times that I've felt more loved than in that moment. And Ben later mentioned to me how important that conversation was for him in broadening his own perspective. Reaching out to a brother or sister with no agenda other than to listen to them share their life experiences is one practical way to develop sympathy for each other.

Other

"Other" could mean a number of different things. It could be ethnically "other," socioeconomically "other," culturally "other," or politically "other." But what I mean is people that we wouldn't necessarily choose as our friends. At least not our first choice. Not out of any hatred or ill-will toward them, but because, as mentioned earlier, we naturally gravitate toward those most like us.

When we pursue the "other" in love, what we'll find is that what we have in common is far greater than anything that separates us. Did you notice how Paul reminded these women about what unites them?

> . . . *help these women, who have labored side by side with me in the gospel together with Clement and the rest of my fellow workers,* **whose names are in the book of life.** *(v. 3)*

Euodia and Syntyche needed to be reminded that, despite whatever was causing their disagreement, they're going to be spending eternity together! Our temptation in the midst of conflict is to highlight our differences and use them as brick and mortar as we construct our walls of separation. Paul was having none of that. Despite our differences, all Christians share in the same heavenly Father, the same Savior, the same Spirit, the same faith, the same hope, the same universal church, the same covenant, the same promises, and the same destiny. Those things are more essential to our being than our ethnicity, our cultural background, or our political party. Let us remember this when we're tempted to "other-ize" Christians we disagree with.

Christ Exemplar

When it comes to affection and sympathy for the "other," as always, the Lord Jesus Christ outshines all in His perfect example. What better model of this do we have than the Lord Jesus Himself? We are more "other" to Jesus than any of us are to each other because of His holy divinity. As the Nicene Creed puts it, Jesus is:

> ... the only Son of God,
>> begotten from the Father before all ages,
>> God from God,
>> Light from Light,
>> true God from true God,
>> begotten, not made;
> of the same essence as the Father.[3]

Before Christ entered this world, we were about as "other" to Him as we could possibly be. Not only because we're creatures and He's the Creator, but more fundamentally because we're *sinful* creatures and He is holy, holy, holy. And yet, out of His infinite treasures of affection and sympathy, He literally entered into our world, our humanity, our suffering. It was His affection and sympathy that caused Him to not count equality with God a thing to be grasped, but to instead empty Himself by taking the form of a servant, being born in the likeness of men. It was His affection and sympathy that caused Him to humble Himself by becoming obedient to the point of death, even death on a cross. After His victorious resurrection, even now He remains our Great High Priest who is able to sympathize with our weaknesses (Heb. 4:15).

Brothers and sisters, by the grace of God, may we have this same mind among ourselves which is ours in Christ Jesus.

Chapter 12

We Got Some Work to Do

Well, we've just about come to the end of the book. If you've made it this far, I want to thank you for spending your valuable time engaging with the ideas I presented here. In chapters 1–3, I shared the story of my background and conversion, showing how God's grace and providence eventually brought me into the mostly White Reformed world. In chapters 4–5, I looked at the divergent views of many Black and White Christians regarding the high profile killings of unarmed Black people by police from 2012 to 2020.

I also explored some of the tainted history of the Reformed church in the area of ethnic injustice and oppression. I looked back at the Protestant Reformation with the goal of answering a simple question: Is there anything inherent in Reformed theology itself that would produce blind spots in its adherents concerning "racism"/ethnic sins? In chapter 6, I argued that the answer to that question is no. I theorized that the problem wasn't the doctrine as much as the social status of those who later embraced Reformed theology. I'll leave it to the historians and scholars to help us further understand that.

In chapters 7–9, my aim was to establish a biblical framework for the discussion, arguing for ethnicity, rather than "race," as the category that most aligns with Scripture. I pointed to the paradigm of the Jew-Gentile conflict in the New Testament and the application of the doctrine of justification by faith alone as two major keys to guide us in our pursuit of ethnic unity. In chapters 10–11, I looked at the biblical call to unity through the lens of Jesus' High Priestly Prayer in John 17 and the apostle Paul's exhortation to Euodia and Syntyche in Philippians 4:2–3.

My goal in this chapter is to leave you with some practical ways to pursue unity with brothers and sisters who hold differing views regarding "race"/ethnicity. I have eight exhortations to help us apply what's been communicated so far.

1. Let us wholeheartedly embrace a new "we."

When God calls a sinner out of darkness into His marvelous light, a radical transformation of the soul occurs that can only properly be referred to as a miracle. To be born again from above is to have one's identity drastically and eternally refashioned. Those who trust in Christ receive a spiritual makeover of monumental proportions. To embrace the gospel is to transition from children of wrath to children of God (Eph. 2:3; John 1:12); from sons of disobedience to sons of the living God (Eph. 5:6; Rom. 9:26); from dead in our sins to new creations in Christ (Eph. 2:1; 2 Cor. 5:17).

When we come to Christ in a saving way, we don't come merely as individuals with our privatized relationship with God. We are brought into a new community; more than that, a new family.

In the most profound way imaginable, the Christian who says "we" means something entirely different post-conversion than she did when she said it before coming to the Lord. The old "we" was limited to our family members, our nationality, our ethnicity, our subcultural group, our political party, our gender, our alma mater, our coworkers, our fellow sports fans, etc. But in Christ, there's a new "we" that supersedes every previous group we once identified with. And this new "we" is diverse. *Extraordinarily diverse.* The new "we" is Black and White, male and female, youthful and elderly, Republican and Democrat, metropolitan and rural. It's scholarly and it lacks formal education. It's blue collar and it's white collar. It's upper class and it's lower class. It's international, it's multilingual, it's multicolored, it's blood-bought, and it's glorious. This is the new "we."

> When we come to Christ in a saving way, we don't come merely as individuals with our privatized relationship with God. We are brought into a new community, a new family.

As the apostle Paul considered the death of Christ and its implications for how Christians see the world, the Holy Spirit prompted him to say:

> *From now on, therefore, we regard no one according to the*
> *flesh. Even though we once regarded Christ according to the*

flesh, we regard him thus no longer. Therefore, if anyone is in Christ, he is a new creation. The old has passed away; behold, the new has come. (2 Cor. 5:16–17)

We regard no one according to the flesh. That is, since Christ died and was raised, we don't see things (or people) from a merely earthly point of view. We are no longer bound to this present evil age (Gal. 1:4). We see things in light of the new creation. If we all would internalize this, the unity of the church would be greatly strengthened.

Take my Blackness, for example. I love being Black, and I'm so thankful God made me this way. I'm also thankful that I was born when and where I was—in close proximity to New York City, the birthplace of hip-hop culture, just as that culture was beginning to develop and expand beyond the five boroughs. I love Black culture, Black women, Black preaching, Black music, Black humor, and the way we season our food. One of the greatest experiences of my life was the first time I went to the National Museum of African American History and Culture in Washington DC with my wife. Seeing the perseverance, resolve, and creativity of my ancestors and our ascension from the dark bowels of slave ships all the way to the Presidency of the United States is humbling and inspiring.

It produces praise in my soul for the God who took what so many meant for evil and instead "meant it for good, to bring it about that many people should be kept alive, as they are today." Think about it. God took what Frederick Douglass referred to as "the corrupt, slaveholding, women-whipping, cradle-plundering, partial and hypocritical Christianity of the land,"[1] and despite that awful distortion, brought many multitudes of Black people in America to Himself with a legacy of faith that has extended for numerous centuries at this point. Only God could do that! And yet, with all that said, in Christ, my primary "we" is not Black people. It's the church. It's the people of God. It's the "saints in the land, . . . the excellent ones, in whom is all my delight" (Ps. 16:3). It's wild to think about, but the reality is that I, a Black, dreaded, hip-hop head from West Philly, have fundamentally more in common with a White coal miner from the mountains of West Virginia, a White stay-at-home mom from South Dakota, or an aging Chinese-American doctor from the Bay Area—if they are Christians—than I have with my Black, hip-hop head cousin from South Philly who doesn't know Christ! This is the glory and beauty of the new humanity.

In my experience as a minority in White majority church settings, one thing I've noticed in my White brothers and sisters is a tendency for many of them to behave as though what they're doing is culturally neutral. By "what they're doing," I'm referring to things like the style of music, the style of preaching, the style of dress, the manner of social interaction, etc. They often fail to recognize that they have a strong culture, and it's not neutral at all. For many, they think something to the effect of, "We're doing it the biblical way. Praise be to God." But when a cultural outsider like me walks into that setting, I think something to the effect of, "They're doing it the 'White' way. And it's biblical. Praise be to God."

There's nothing wrong with doing it the "White" way, of course. Provided it's in line with Scripture and brings glory to God. The problem is when one conflates what's cultural with what's biblical in a way that reinforces blind spots and creates barriers to participation for those outside the majority culture. Late Westminster Seminary professor Harvie Conn warned against this tendency back in the 1980s when he noted that contextualization is "the art of planting the gospel seed in a culture's diverse soils without also planting the flower pot."[2] One way that the majority culture can embrace the new "we" is to strive to be sensitive to cultural outsiders in their midst and even be willing to make changes to how things are done for the sake of greater unity through diversity in the church.

We all have our temptations in this area. My sinful temptation is to glory in my God-given Blackness in a way that eclipses my "in Christ-ness." When I do so, I'm getting things terribly backwards. It's the glory of being in Christ that should shine the brightest in my life. My Blackness is just a facet on the jewel. Christ is the penetrating Light that shines on the jewel, allowing its beauty to be seen in its proper place among all the other facets. Apart from the Light, the facet on the jewel and the jewel itself are hidden and dormant, providing no delight to the eye whatsoever. May we appreciate the facet and praise God for the facet while never treasuring the facet over the Light that makes it attractive.

2. Let us keep the gospel central.

In the flurry of dialogue about "race" and justice over the past few years, the person and work of Jesus Christ has often been relegated to the background. This must not be. There's a reason why Scripture refers to the gospel as that which is of first importance (1 Cor. 15:3). When it says that, it doesn't mean that there aren't other important things to talk about. But what it does mean is that those other important things are not meant to be our primary focus in such a way that the gospel loses its centrality. Satan is crafty, and he specializes in tempting Christians to distort two complementary truths by focusing on one and disregarding the other.

So, on the one hand, he'll tempt some believers to say, "What's all this social justice stuff? Just preach the gospel!" Doing justice and preaching the gospel are both biblical imperatives (Mic. 6:8; Prov. 21:3; 1 Cor. 9:16). When they are pitted against each other, the byproduct is Christians that follow in the footsteps of the Pharisees, who traveled across land and sea to make converts but neglected the "weightier matters of the law: justice and mercy and faithfulness" (Matt. 23:15, 23). On the other hand, he'll tempt other believers to get so consumed with the pursuit of earthly justice that they lose sight of the certainty of divine justice (Nah. 1:2–3), forgetting that God is both just and the one who is able to justify the oppressed and the oppressor through faith in Jesus Christ. May the life, death, and resurrection of Christ be the thing we shout the loudest even as we rightly give voice to its implications.

> Satan is crafty, and he specializes in tempting Christians to distort two complementary truths by focusing on one and disregarding the other.

3. Let us be countercultural in how we pursue unity with Christians whom we disagree with.

When the gospel is central in my life, it shapes how I interact with Christians I disagree with. It means that I don't have to demonize other Christians. It means I can speak the truth in love, with kindness, gentleness, and respect. We don't have the right to cast off the fruit of the Spirit in the name of standing for truth. Malice, spite, argumentativeness, sarcastic mockery, belittling, and mean-spiritedness should not be named among the people of God at all, but especially when dealing with other believers. For Christians with or without large followings to regularly display this kind of behavior in public for the whole world to observe is shameful and dishonors the name of Christ. May God give us the grace to choose the better way urged by our brother Peter, who knew a thing or two about putting his foot in his mouth:

> *Finally, all of you, have unity of mind, sympathy, brotherly love, a tender heart, and a humble mind. (1 Peter 3:8)*

4. Let us assume the best about our brothers and sisters.

In order for any relationship to truly thrive, mutual trust is essential. When Satan came along in the garden of Eden, he introduced distrust with his very first recorded words. First, it was distrust for God. That eventually led to horizontal distrust. In both cases, relational brokenness was the inevitable result. When it comes to the pursuit of ethnic unity, suspicion and distrust are very difficult roadblocks to overcome. In order for real progress to be made, we must assume the best about our brothers and sisters in Christ.

For Black Christians, that may mean fighting against the impulse to assume that the White brother or sister who disagrees with you does so only because of their "racism." For White Christians, it may mean fighting against the impulse to assume that Black brothers and sisters who are concerned about ethnic justice have abandoned the gospel. This is where having real-life relationships with Christians of different ethnicities and perspectives is very important. As we are truly involved in each other's lives, that shared experience will help build the trust that can be beneficial to lean on when the time comes to work through our differences. The local church is the best context for this. Which brings me to my next exhortation.

5. Let us enter each other's worlds.

This relates to what I wrote in the last chapter concerning affection and sympathy. There is a connection between sympathy and proximity. It's much more difficult to sympathize or develop deep affection from a distance. Affection and sympathy are best cultivated within the context of real-life relationships.

There's a younger White couple who are members of our church in Philly. My wife and I meet with them regularly and they have become dear friends. As I write this, our church is about 53 percent Black, 35 percent White and 10 percent Asian and Latino. The wife, Sarah, grew up in an urban area in a large city in the Northeast. For her, multiethnic interaction was a regular part of her life growing up. The husband, Dave, grew up in an extremely rural area in the Midwest that was almost all White. He rarely, if ever, interacted with Black people. He recently shared with us that when he first came to our church, he didn't realize just how much his worldview had been shaped by his upbringing. It's only as he's entered into in-depth relationships with people from other backgrounds that his perspective has changed on a number of different issues.

I helped Dave and Sarah move into their first apartment when they moved to Philly. They have been in our home and babysat our kids while Blair and I have gone on date nights. We've shared meals together. We've prayed and worshiped the Lord together. We counseled them through various trials they've had as a young married couple. Dave and I have had in-depth conversations about family, finances, and the future. Blair and Sarah have shared their hearts with each other. We've spoken openly and honestly about hard topics like "race" and politics. In other words, we've done life together.

So, now, when an unarmed Black man is killed by the police, they have a different perspective than what they may have had when they first came to the church. It doesn't mean that the conclusions they draw about a particular case will necessarily be different. But it does mean that when they think of Black men, it's not merely theoretical to them. Their first thought is not a news report or statistics from a website. They have particular people that they know and love dearly in mind. That makes a difference. They're able to sympathize in a way that they wouldn't be able to in the same way had there not been the same proximity. The "one anothers" of the New Testament assume that we're in each other's lives enough to walk them out. Consider some of the things the church is commanded to do:

Welcome one another (Rom. 15:7)
Encourage one another (1 Thess. 5:11; Heb. 3:13)
Be devoted to one another (Rom. 12:10a)
Build up one another (Rom. 14:19)
Admonish one another (Col. 3:16)
Comfort one another (2 Cor. 13:11)
Care for one another (1 Cor. 12:25)
Bear with one another (Eph. 4:2)
Confess faults to one another (James 5:16)
Forgive one another (Eph. 4:32)
Show hospitality to one another (1 Peter 4:9)

The best way to live these out is by being in close proximity with each other. As we seek to love each other and, by God's grace, walk in these commands, the Spirit works in our hearts to produce affection and sympathy for our brothers and sisters from different ethnic backgrounds.

I recognize that many people live in areas that are more homogenous, which makes proximity to Christians from different ethnicities difficult, if not impossible. People in that situation may need to apply these principles to those of the same ethnicity who may be "other" in different ways (political views, theological perspective, socioeconomic background, education level, etc.).

6. Let us deal graciously with each other's faults.

The biblical commands to bear with one another (Eph. 4:2) and to forgive one another (Eph. 4:32) assume that there will be times when we sin against each other. This is true in all of life, so we shouldn't expect it to be different when dealing with a subject as inflammatory as "race" is in America. If we're seeking to maintain the unity of the Spirit in the bond of peace, we're going to need extra measures of grace for each other. For Black Christians, this may mean giving our White brothers and sisters room to make mistakes in conversations without flying off the handle or terminating the relationship because we're so easily offended.

Some White Christians are so afraid of saying the wrong thing that they walk on eggshells in conversations with their Black friends, or they disengage entirely out of fear. For example, how does a White person refer to a Black person? Is it "Black"? African American? Person of color? If I'm ready to snap on somebody because I prefer one of those rather than the other two, that puts my White friend in a tough position because they basically have a 66 percent chance of offending me, depending on their word choice. For the record, Black people view this differently, sometimes based on generation. Personally, I don't mind any of those. As long as you stay away from "Afro-American" (an Afro is a haircut), "colored" (wait, what year is this?), or "negro" (???), we're good. The best thing is to simply ask, "Do you prefer one term over another?" There needs to be grace for things like this.

My need to be gracious toward my White brothers and sisters was brought home to me in a way I'll never forget a few years back. Blair and I went to a Christian conference in another city. While we were there, an older White sister in the Lord took the initiative to approach us and introduce herself. As we talked, we realized that we lived in the same area. She was faithful to keep in touch with us and very encouraging to me regarding my music ministry. One day, she organized a dinner for us. She went out of her way to fill an entire restaurant with family and friends from her church. We were the guests of honor. We met at a location close to the restaurant and walked there together. As we walked and talked, she said, "So many people are really excited to meet you! When we get there, you're going to be sitting at the table with Leroy and the judge." (I'm sure she said the name of "the judge," but it was loud where we were walking and all I heard was "the judge." You'll see why this is important momentarily.)

When we got to the restaurant, it was packed with a sea of smiling white faces. Honestly, it was overwhelming. As a natural introvert, it made me really uncomfortable. Our table was all the way in the back. As I awkwardly made my way through the crowd, waving and shaking hands like the president at a fundraiser, I spotted the only other brown face in the restaurant and made eye contact with him. He was seated at our table. When I got there, he stood up to greet me. With all the enthusiasm I could muster, I reached out, shook his hand, and, just to make sure he could hear me in the crowded room, I exclaimed in an unnaturally loud voice, "What's up, Leroy?" He looked back at me, and in a full-on deadpan voice said, "My name is Stephen." The White guy who was seated a few seats down from Stephen said, "Hey, Shai, I'm Leroy."

If I were White, my face would have turned beet-red. I said, "I'm so sorry, man." I was so embarrassed! Thankfully, he was really gracious about it, and we went on with our evening. As I thought about it, my shame was compounded. I had made two assumptions. One was reasonable, the other wasn't. My first assumption was that the Black guy had to be Leroy because, I mean, come on. How many White Leroys do you know? The second assumption was more inexcusable. When I saw the Black guy, it didn't enter into my mind that he might actually be the judge. What a ridiculous assumption on my part. When I look at my friends, I'm surrounded by Black excellence. My closest Black friends are college professors, pastors, high school principals, educators, authors, lawyers, and business owners. And yet, here I was making foolish assumptions based on stereotypes. If that's possible for *me* to do, I have to give grace to my White brothers and sisters who may have very little exposure to Black people and make similar kinds of assumptions.

In the years since that incident, Blair and I have actually become good friends with Leroy and his wife. We've also been blessed to spend time with "the judge" and his beautiful family. Whenever I think about that story, I laugh out loud as I'm reminded of how

God puts up with my foolishness. Surely, I can extend that same grace to others.

7. Let us persevere.

I can personally testify that the fight for ethnic unity in the church is exhausting. There is so much hurt, so many misunderstandings, so much talking past each other. It can often be discouraging and feel like very little progress is being made. The easy thing to do would be to limit our interactions to those we're most comfortable with and wait until glory for things to get better. But is that what God calls us to? By no means! God calls us to something much greater: love. There's nothing ambiguous about how the Lord commanded His disciples in His final instructions to them:

> "A new commandment I give to you, that you love one
> another: just as I have loved you, you also are to love one
> another." (John 13:34)

We're called to love each other as Jesus loved us. And how has He done that? He loved us by laying down His life for us on the cross (John 15:13). He loves us at the present moment by interceding on our behalf (Heb. 7:25). He also loves us by exercising great patience toward us each day (1 Tim. 1:16). Jesus doesn't give up on us when we're slow to change. He continues to bear with us. The apostle Paul reminds us what love looks like in this case:

> Love bears all things, believes all things, hopes all
> things, endures all things. (1 Cor. 13:7)

The pursuit of ethnic unity is a marathon, not a sprint. This problem didn't develop overnight. The division between Black and White Christians in America is centuries in the making. It's shortsighted and naive of us to think the issue will be resolved with a conference, a sermon series, or a few articles. Those things have their place, but we need to think long-term regarding this fight for unity. One thing I know for sure: if we try to do it in our own strength, we will fail and burn out in the process. Victory in this spiritual battle is going to be won on our knees. The prayer of the apostle Paul for the Colossians is instructive for us. Among other things, he prayed that they would be "strengthened with all power, according to his glorious might, for all endurance and patience with joy" (Col. 1:11).

The pursuit of ethnic unity is a marathon, not a sprint.

That's what we need. The power and glorious might of our God. When we feel weary in the struggle, we can pray for endurance. When we're tempted toward bitterness or anger toward our brother or sister of another ethnicity, we can pray that God would grant us patience. And not the grit-your-teeth-while-you're-still-mad-on-the-inside kind of patience. No. Patience *with joy*. And what is the basis of that joy in the midst of all the discouraging things we see on social media from Christians regarding "race," for example? Well, we'll just let Paul finish his thought:

> . . . *giving thanks to the Father, who has qualified you to share in the inheritance of the saints in light. He has delivered us from the domain of darkness and transferred us to the kingdom of his beloved Son, in whom we have redemption, the forgiveness of sins. (Col. 1:12–14)*

Ah, there it is! It's gospel hope that fuels present joy. It's knowing that God has forgiven all my ethnic sins as well as the ethnic sins of my brothers and sisters in Christ that enables me to rejoice as we work through hard conversations together. It's my awareness that through adoption, God is our Father and that we've been purchased from our slavery to sin and that we share in the same inheritance that fills my heart with gladness even if we have to keep asking each other for forgiveness as we stumble along this slippery road together. Apart from Jesus, we can do nothing. But through Him, we can do all things. Since by the grace of God we have Him, let us persevere.

8. Let us remember Jesus Christ.

"Remember Jesus Christ, risen from the dead, the offspring of David, as preached in my gospel" (2 Tim. 2:8). The idea of "remembering" is a continual theme in Scripture. That's because we all suffer from spiritual amnesia. That is, we learn things and then, because of our sin, we forget what we learned and have to be reminded over and over. As the apostle Paul sat in a Roman prison, preparing for his imminent death, what did he want his protégé Timothy to remember? Jesus Christ. When he said "remember," it wasn't passive. He wasn't simply saying don't forget. He was telling Timothy to be proactive in engaging his mind. He had just told him a verse earlier to "think over what I say."

We naturally call things to mind on a regular basis. Whether it's for work, school, family, business, or leisure, we're fixing our minds on different things regularly. Paul is telling Timothy to fix his mind on Jesus Christ. As we consider how to pursue ethnic unity, it may seem counterintuitive, but we must fix our minds on

Jesus as we do so in order for our pursuit to be fruitful. So exactly what is it that we should remember?

Remember His Glorious Person

Remember that Jesus is the eternal Son of God, God over all, blessed forever, Amen.

Remember that He is the Word who was in the beginning with God and who was God.

Remember that He is equal in essence with the Father.

Remember that all that can be said about the Father's divine nature can properly be said about the Son as well.

As the old school catechism put it, God is

> . . . infinite in being and perfection . . . immutable, immense, eternal, incomprehensible, almighty, most wise, most holy, most free, most absolute; working all things according to the counsel of His own immutable and most righteous will, for His own glory; most loving, gracious, merciful, long-suffering, abundant in goodness and truth.[3]

These things are all true of God the Father and they're also true of God the Son.

This is why when Jesus quieted the storm in Matthew 14:33, and it tells us, "those in the boat worshiped him, saying, 'Truly you are the Son of God,'" Jesus did not stop them. This is why Jesus said in John 5:21, "As the Father raises the dead and gives them life, so also the Son gives life to whom he will." This is why Jesus said in John 14:9, "Whoever has seen me has seen the Father." This is why Jesus said in John 8:58, "Before Abraham was, I am." Remember that this eternal Word became flesh, so that not only is Jesus the Son of God, but He's also the Son of Man. 100% God, 100% man. Two natures united in one glorious Person. Remember that in His incarnation, as John Owen said, "He became what He was not, but He ceased not to be what He was."[4] As the hymn puts it, "David's Son, yet David's Lord."[5] Remember His glorious Person.

Remember His Preexistence

Remember that Jesus is eternal. His appearance in the womb of the Virgin Mary was not the beginning of His existence. As the divine Son of God, Jesus is from everlasting to everlasting. He has eternally enjoyed the fullness of joy in His Father's presence (Ps. 16:11). As Jesus prayed in John 17:5: "And now, Father, glorify me in your own presence with the glory that I had with you *before the world existed.*"

Remember His Perfect Life

Remember that Jesus fulfilled God's law perfectly. Internally and externally. Every thought that Jesus had was a sinless thought, every word that He spoke was a sinless word, every deed He performed was a sinless deed. "He committed no sin, neither was deceit found in his mouth" (1 Peter 2:22).

Remember His Sacrificial Death

Remember that on the cross, Jesus suffered the full weight of the fury and wrath of God against sin. Remember that He laid down His life as a substitute in place of all who would trust Him, including you if you would trust Him even now. As 1 Peter 2:24 says, "He himself bore our sins in his body on the tree."

Remember His Glorious Resurrection

Remember that Jesus didn't stay in the tomb, but that on the third day He rose from the grave. Remember that Jesus has conquered Satan, sin, and death. Remember that Jesus "abolished death and brought life and immortality to light through the gospel" (2 Tim. 1:10).

Remember Jesus in Every Situation

When you're tempted to sin, remember Jesus Christ, that "he himself has suffered when tempted, he is able to help those who are being tempted" (Heb. 2:18). When you've fallen into sin, remember Jesus Christ, that He is our "advocate with the Father, Jesus Christ the righteous [and that] he is the propitiation for our sins" (1 John 2:1–2). When someone has sinned against you, remember Jesus Christ, that He "endured from sinners such hostility against himself, so that you may not grow weary or fainthearted" (Heb. 12:3). When you're discouraged, remember Jesus Christ, who said "in the world you will have tribulation. But take heart; I have overcome the world" (John 16:33).

There is much work to be done in the pursuit of ethnic unity. We need the help of the Holy Spirit to sustain us and give us endurance. So brothers and sisters, let us look "to Jesus, the founder and perfecter of our faith, who for the joy that was set before him endured the cross, despising the shame, and is seated at the right hand of the throne of God" (Heb. 12:2).

As we do so, may the church walk in unity, may our witness to the world be strengthened, and may God be glorified. Amen.

Soon and Very Soon

One of Rev. Dr. Martin Luther King Jr.'s most famous statements is that Sunday morning at 11 a.m. is the most segregated hour in America. As I write this, it has been more than half a century since King made those remarks. While we may have made some progress since the sixties up until a few years ago, the last few years seem to have widened the divide that was already there. For whatever reason, it seems as if the church in the US has been either unable or unwilling to overcome "America's Original Sin." One sobering observation that ought to humble us and grieve us is that some of the sociological factors that contribute to the divide actually haven't changed much since slavery.[1]

Many Christians who have made valiant efforts toward "racial reconciliation" for decades are throwing in the towel and treating the pursuit of ethnic unity in the church like family and friends treat their heroin-addicted loved one after the interventions hit double digits and the relapses continue. "We love him, and would love to see him change, but he has to want it for himself. We'll be there for him should he get better, but for now, the best thing for him and us is to separate and create some healthy boundaries." I understand the exhaustion; I really do. Most of the time, this is the last thing I want to talk about. Part of my writing this book was to help me think more clearly about this topic so that I might organize some of the fragmented thoughts that have been whirling around in my mind for many years. But engaging those with whom we disagree on this issue in a way that preserves unity can often be discouraging. The toxicity of the public discourse just adds to the frustration.

But This I Call to Mind . . .

With all that being said, the subtitle of this book is *Finding Hope in the Fight for Ethnic Unity* because I really am hopeful. One reason for my hopefulness is something I alluded to in chapter 10. In Jesus' prayer in John 17:21–22, He prayed that the church would be one. I argued that the Father always answers Jesus' prayers. Because of that, we can be assured that the unity of the church will be accomplished. It was purchased at the cross. We seek to walk in it now, knowing that it will be perfected in eternity. That brings me to the second reason for my hopefulness, which is that we know the end of the story. I'm the type of person who enjoys watching the same movie more than once. Some movies reward the viewer for making the time investment of multiple viewings. *The Sixth Sense,*[2] directed by Philadelphia-area native M. Night Shyamalan, is one such film. The premise, hidden in plain sight during the story, is brilliantly revealed at the end of the movie, which makes watching it again an entirely new experience. You see it through new eyes now that you know the ending. Well, when it comes to ethnic unity between Christians, we don't have to wait for the surprise reveal at the end of the story. We already know.

A Great Multitude

In Revelation we are told of a glorious scene in heaven:

> *After this I looked, and behold, a great multitude that no one could number, from every nation, from all tribes and peoples and languages, standing before the throne and before the Lamb, clothed in white robes, with palm branches in their hands, and crying out with a loud voice, "Salvation belongs to our God who sits on the throne, and to the Lamb!"*
> *(Rev. 7:9–10)*

What was lost in Eden is now exponentially found in Paradise. This is the unspeakable good that God meant from the evil of Babel. This is the gospel that God preached to Abraham. This is God's promise to the patriarchs fulfilled in spectacular fashion. This is the risen and exalted Lord Jesus Christ receiving the reward for His suffering. This is what Pentecost foreshadowed. And now, at last, it all makes sense. The sin, the pain, the misery, the tears, the suffering, the death. It really did have a purpose. Let God be true and every man a liar. All that God has promised has found its "yes" and "amen" in Christ. God has sent out His angels with a loud trumpet call, and they have gathered His elect from the four winds, from one end of heaven to the other.

All that the Father has given to Jesus have come to Him, and they have not been cast out. Jesus has done the will of the Father. Jesus has lost none of all that the Father has given Him, but has raised them up on the last day. Many have come from east and west to recline at table with Abraham, Isaac, and Jacob in the kingdom of heaven. The end has come, when Jesus has delivered the kingdom to God the Father after destroying every rule and every authority and power. Jesus has reigned until He has put all His enemies under His feet. Satan has been thrown into the lake of fire and sulfur where the beast and the false prophet were, and they will be tormented day and night forever and ever. Death, the last enemy, has been destroyed. Let the eternal celebration begin!

Unity in Diversity

Notice the diversity. What lavish and abundant diversity! Every nation. All tribes. All peoples. All languages. All ethnicities. Not one left out. How could they be? The gospel of the kingdom has been proclaimed throughout the whole world as a testimony to all nations that the end has come. Here we are. Don't be mistaken. This is not diversity for diversity's sake. Ethnic diversity is not virtuous in and of itself. Hell is also a very diverse place. The most glorious expression of ethnic diversity is a redeemed humanity united around the beauty of Jesus Christ, whose blood ransomed people for God from every tribe, language, people, and nation. This is not inclusiveness to meet a quota or to make the front of a college brochure look better. This is diversity with a divine purpose: to show off the glory of God to the entire universe as the Light of the world shines magnificently upon every facet of the jewel of a redeemed humanity.

Notice the unity. What devout and passionate unity! A countless multitude all on the same page. No one out of step. No one doing their own thing. No one trying to outshine anybody else. How could they be? They're in the unveiled presence of God and the Lamb! When the sun comes out, all the stars disappear. There's no place for a superstar in the same universe that has Jesus in it. Don't be mistaken. This is not unity for unity's sake. Unity is not virtuous in itself. Hell is also a very unified place. Hell is Babel spun out and unraveled to its ghastly conclusion. Wicked people opposed to God futilely trying to ambush the heavens and make a name for themselves in their pride and arrogance.

Notice the diversity. What lavish and abundant diversity! Every nation. All tribes. All peoples. All languages. All ethnicities.

The most glorious expression of unity is exactly what we see here. A multitude of diverse, blood-bought saints doing exactly what they were created to do: praise God with all their might. This is the unmitigated joy of a people for God's namesake in lockstep unison. All washed by the blood of the Lamb. All holy and clothed in the spotless righteousness of Christ. All humbled before God with a posture of unabashed worship and adoration. All carrying symbols of victory and salvation. All lifting their glorified voices in fervent praise. All empowered by the Spirit to exult in the kingship of God and the sacrifice of the Savior.

This is why I'm hopeful. The story has already been written. The end is known from the beginning. All the ethnic strife and division we experience in the world is a mere footnote in the index of history. This too shall pass. In the meantime, we have a great opportunity. Very rarely do people consciously have a chance to change the narrative of an entire tradition for the better.

Semper Reformanda

This is why I speak of a New Reformation. Not new in the sense that the doctrine needs to change. By no means! Scripture alone. Grace alone. Faith alone. Christ alone. The glory of God alone. The doctrines of grace. The doctrine of justification. The God of the covenants. These are ancient landmarks that should never be moved (Prov. 22:28). These are hills to plant flags on and die on, if need be. When I say new, I mean new in terms of the makeup of the Reformed community. It's more about a *who* than a *what*. The New Reformation looks more like Revelation 7:9 than the Westminster Assembly (as grateful as we all are for the Westminster Assembly!).

The New Reformation is a group of Black, White, Latino, and Asian men in the basement of a church in ungentrified North Philly reading through *The Godly Man's Picture* by Thomas Watson together.

The New Reformation is men and women who are just as familiar with Trip Lee and Jackie Hill-Perry as they are with Isaac Watts and John Newton.

The New Reformation is a sixty-something-year-old Christian woman with a Jewish background sitting with a group of twenty-

and thirty-something-year-old Black and Brown women and sharing her reflections on years of studies in the complete works of John Owen.

The New Reformation is a multiethnic squad of college-age Christians and young adults who crave expository preaching, are serious about orthodoxy and orthopraxy, hunger and thirst for righteousness, and love Christian hip-hop.

The New Reformation is gospel-saturated, theologically astute women who know their Bibles, know their God, and use their gifts for the building up of the body of Christ.

The New Reformation is planting multiethnic churches led by Black and Brown pastors in the inner cities of New York City, Atlanta, Chicago, Los Angeles, Hampton, Virginia, Philadelphia, St. Louis, and Washington, DC.

The New Reformation is systematic and biblical theologies by African and Asian pastors and scholars included in the curriculums of seminaries and Bible colleges in the US and the UK.

The New Reformation is declaring the lordship of Christ and the kingdom of God through word and deed.

The New Reformation is urban and suburban believers who embrace their identity as strangers and pilgrims and therefore refuse to allow their Christianity to be co-opted by partisan politics.

The New Reformation is preaching and speaking out about a biblical view of marriage, a biblical view of ethnic injustice, a biblical view of justice for the unborn, and a biblical view of caring for the poor and marginalized without regard to how the surrounding secular society categorizes those particular concerns politically.[3]

The New Reformation is diverse. *Extraordinarily diverse.* The New Reformation is Black and White, male and female, youthful and elderly, Republican and Democrat, metropolitan and rural. It's scholarly and it lacks formal education. It's blue collar and it's white collar. It's upper class and it's lower class. It's international, it's multilingual, it's multicolored, it's blood-bought, and it's glorious. This is the New Reformation.

Soli Deo Gloria.

George Floyd and Me

As a Christian hip-hop artist, I've had the privilege of proclaiming Christ in my music for many years now. One of the encouraging and surprising aspects of that journey has been seeing how the Lord has used music to make connections across ethnic lines. Before the recent pandemic, a Christian hip-hop concert was often a beautiful picture of the diversity of the new earth, with people from many walks of life united around the message of Christ and Him crucified. On many occasions, I've marveled at the reality of me, a Black man from Philly who grew up steeped in hip-hop culture, united with brothers and sisters of different ethnicities, ages, and cultures as we fix our eyes on Jesus together.

Over the years, I've heard from many people that they were affected by the truth contained in my music, even though hip-hop wasn't their natural cultural preference. Whenever I heard this,

I was struck by the power and beauty of like-mindedness. It was clear to me that we were like-minded concerning particular emphases in the music—the glory of God, the supremacy of Christ, the centrality of the cross, and the importance of biblical theology. By God's grace, I will fight for all of those things until the Lord takes me home.

But one of the painful things I've discovered over the last several years or so since Trayvon Martin's killing is that it's possible to agree on those things and yet be in a completely different place when it comes to the issue of racial injustice. Just because I've made an intentional decision to focus on that which is "of first importance" (1 Cor. 15:3) doesn't mean there aren't other important things that need to be addressed in the church. It also doesn't mean that being a Christian has exempted me from the reality of being a Black man in America and all the stigma that comes with it.

Empathy, Understanding, Unity

In the aftermath of George Floyd's killing, my wife and I received an email from a White sister in Christ. I was hesitant to let her know how I was feeling for fear of being misunderstood and, frankly, because of emotional exhaustion. But as I began to write, I poured out my heart in a way I've never really articulated all at once. I've been encouraged by some around me to share this publicly.

In doing so, I understand that I don't speak for all Black people on this issue, though many can resonate with my experience. I also recognize the risk that comes with putting yourself out there and being vulnerable in the age of social media, online trolls, and keyboard vigilantes. But if this can help promote any empathy, understanding, and unity in the body of Christ, it's more than worth it. Here is what I shared with her:

Sister, I'm going to tell you how I'm doing. And as I tell you, please understand that I'm incapable of completing this message without weeping. There's a part of me that's saying, "Spare yourself the pain, Shai. It's not worth it." But I'm choosing not to listen to that part of me because I would be robbing you of an opportunity to "bear one another's burdens" and "mourn with those who mourn"—and I'm sure, as a sister in Christ, you want to do just that.

Sister, I am heartbroken and devastated. I feel gutted. I haven't been able to focus on much at all since I saw the horrific video of George Floyd's murder. The image of that officer with hand in pocket as he calmly and callously squeezed the life out of that man while he begged for his life is an image that will haunt me until the day I die. But it's not just the video of this one incident. For many Black people, it's never about just one incident. Just as it wasn't just about the videos of Eric Garner, Tamir Rice, Philando Castile, Sandra Bland, Laquan McDonald, Walter Scott, Rodney King, etc., etc., etc., etc.

This is about how being a Black man in America has shaped both the way I see myself and the way others have seen me my whole life. It's about being told to leave the sneaker store as a 12-year-old, because I was taking too long to decide which sneakers I wanted to buy with my birthday money and the White saleswoman assumed I was in the store to steal something.

It's about being handcuffed and thrown into the back of a police car while walking down the street during college, and then waiting for a White couple to come identify whether or not I was the one who'd committed a crime against them, knowing that if they said I was the one, I would be immediately taken to jail, no questions asked.

It's about walking down the street as a young man and beginning to notice that White people, women especially, would cross to the other side of the street to avoid walking past me—and me beginning to preemptively cross to the other side myself to save them the trouble of being afraid and to save me the humiliation of that silent transaction.

It's about taking a road trip with my sons to visit Blair's family in Michigan—and my greatest fear being getting pulled over for no reason other than driving while Black, told to get out of the car, cuffed, and sat down on the side of the road, utterly emasculated and humiliated with my young boys looking out the window, terrified, which is exactly what happened to a good friend of mine when he took his family on a road trip.

It's about the exhaustion of constantly feeling I have to assert my humanity in front of some White people I'm meeting for the first time, to let them know, "Hey! I'm not a threat! You don't need to be afraid. If you got to know me, I'm sure we have things in common!"

It's about me sometimes asking my wife to do things in certain customer-service situations, since I know she'll likely get treated better than I will.

It's about borrowing a baby swing from a White friend in our mostly White suburb of DC and her telling me, "Sure, you can borrow it. I have to step out, but I'll leave it on the porch for you. Just go grab it"—and then feeling heart palpitations as my car approached her home, debating whether or not to get the swing and being terrified as I walked up the steps that someone would think I was stealing it and call the cops on me.

It's about intentionally making sure the carseats are in the car, even if the kids aren't, so that when (not "if"—it happens all the time) I'm stopped by the police, they will perhaps notice the carseats and also the wedding band on one of my visible hands on the wheel (which I've been taught to keep there and not move until he tells me to—and even then, in an exaggeratedly slow manner) and will perhaps think, "This man is married with a family and small kids like me. Maybe he wants to get home safely to his family just like I do."

It's about having to explain to my four-year-old son at his mostly White Christian school that the kids who laughed at him for having brown skin were wrong, that God made him in His image, and that his skin is beautiful—after he told me, "Daddy, I don't want brown skin. I want white skin."

It's about having what feels like genuine fellowship with my White brothers and sisters who share the same Reformed theology—until I mention racism, injustice, or police brutality, at which point I'm looked at skeptically as if I embrace a "social gospel" or am some kind of "liberal" or "social justice warrior."

And it's about sometimes feeling like some of my White friends aren't that particularly interested in truly knowing me—at least not in any meaningful way that might actually challenge their preconceptions. Rather, it feels like they use me to feel better about themselves because I check off the "Black friend" box. Much more could be mentioned. These were the first things that came to mind.

So when I watch a video like George Floyd's, it represents for me the fresh reopening of a deep wound and the reliving of layers of trauma that get exponentially compounded each time a well-meaning White friend says, "All lives matter." Of course they do, but in this country, Black lives have been treated like they don't matter for centuries and present inequities in criminal justice, income, housing, health care, education, etc., show that all lives don't actually matter like they should.

So, whenever someone asks how I'm doing with everything going on, this is some of what I bring to the table. And it's a big part of the picture of who Shai Linne is.

Grieving, But with Hope

But it's not the whole picture. Though I'm deeply grieved, I am not without hope. Personally, I have little confidence in our government or policymakers to change the systemic factors that contributed to the George Floyd situation. But my hope isn't in the government. My hope is in the Lord. In a different context, the prophet Jeremiah said some things that resonate with me as I process this: "I remember my affliction and my wandering, the bitterness and the gall. I well remember them, and my soul is downcast within me" (Lam. 3:19–20 NIV).

I love that the prophet doesn't minimize the pain or act like it isn't real. There are three whole chapters of "bitterness and gall"—and no trite clichés wrapped in theological terms. Jeremiah acknowledges how much it hurts and, as a result, his soul is downcast. Too often when people are hurting, we can play the role of Job's friends, saying things that may be theologically true while adding to our suffering friend's pain. One of the most hurtful things we can do is to make mourners justify their pain.

Jeremiah gives thoughtful meditation to the trauma he has experienced at the hand of the Lord. But then he does something remarkable in the next verse. He preaches to himself!

> *Yet this I call to mind*
>   *and therefore I have hope:*
>
> *Because of the* LORD's *great love we are not consumed,*
>   *for his compassions never fail.*
> *They are new every morning;*
>   *great is your faithfulness.*
> *I say to myself, "The* LORD *is my portion;*
>   *therefore I will wait for him." (Lam. 3:21–24* NIV)

Jeremiah makes a conscious decision to think about something that fuels his hope: God's character. He considers God's "great love," God's "compassion," and God's "faithfulness." He reminds himself that the Lord is his portion. Jeremiah knows he and Israel deserve to be consumed because of their sin—but he also knows that the God who disciplines is the God who saves (v. 26).

Life as "Usual"

So, brothers and sisters, in a nutshell, I'm so thankful for Jesus. I deserve to be consumed, but I'm not, because of God's compassion. That's what the cross and resurrection are all about. My pain and trauma are real. But my salvation, in a sense, is even more real, because my pain and trauma are temporary. My salvation is eternal.

This is why I choose to focus on what I do in my music. It's the glory of God, the supremacy of Jesus Christ, the centrality of the cross, and biblical theology that put my experience as a Black man in America into its proper perspective.

I hope I'm not giving in to skepticism or pessimism, but I firmly believe that unless the systemic problems with policing and the criminal justice system are addressed, we're going to continue to see these kinds of things for years to come. My fear is that the attention garnered by the protests will eventually die down (as it always does), and then my White friends will go right back to "life as usual."

But I don't have that luxury.

For me, "life as usual" means recognizing some people perceive me as a threat based solely on the color of my skin. For me, "life as usual" means preparing my sons for the coming time when they're no longer perceived as cute little boys, but teenage "thugs." Long after George Floyd disappears from the headlines, I will still be a Black man in America.

And you know what? I thank God for that! He knew exactly what He was doing when He made me the way He did. Despite the real and exhausting challenges that come with my outward packaging, I know that I'm fearfully and wonderfully made. And I wouldn't want to be anything other than what I am: a follower of Jesus Christ who has been saved by grace and redeemed by the blood of the Lamb—who also has brown skin and dreadlocks and does hip-hop. And God has chosen, in His great mercy, to leverage it all for His glory. Praise be to Him.

Acknowledgments

Thanks to my lovely bride, Blair. This book would not have been possible without your love, your help, your friendship, your correction, and your suggestions. Thank you for holding it down when I was working long days and nights, going on writing retreats, and struggling through the stress of writer's block. Your godliness is a constant encouragement and challenge to me. The beauty, grace, and finesse that God crafted you with are a daily reminder that our God loves and lavishes His grace upon the undeserving.

Thanks to my beautiful children Sage, Maya, and Ezra. You don't understand the complexities of this book right now, but I pray that someday when you're older, you'll pick this up, learn a little more than you knew about your dad, and most importantly, be pointed to the Savior, who was intentional when He made you the way He did and when He died and rose the way He did.

Thanks to my mom for praying me into the kingdom!

Thanks to my sister Shenita. The work of transformation that the Lord has done in you has been one of the most encouraging things I've witnessed as a believer. I'm so grateful for you!

Thanks to all the saints at RCF. It's been such a blessing to worship and serve the Lord with y'all. Y'all are "the saints in the land. . . the excellent ones, in whom is all my delight" (Ps. 16:3).

Thanks to Mark Dever, the elders, and the congregation at CHBC. Thanks to Garrett Kell, the elders, and the congregation at DRBC.

Thanks to all who played a part in Lamp Mode Recordings. In eternity, we'll get a better sense of the fruit that the Lord produced in those early years. May the Lord keep us faithful to Him beyond the music!

Thanks to all my guys: Duce, Derek, Joel, Miguel, Brady, Josh, Ant, T. J., Brian Davis, and Brian Dye. Your friendship has truly blessed me. The convos we've had over the years have helped shape many of the ideas in this book.

Thanks to my editors Drew Dyck and Amanda Cleary Eastep, as well as the entire staff at Moody Publishers. Drew, you were really gracious and patient with me as I kept extending my deadlines. And Amanda, thank you for your, umm . . . meticulousness (smile). This book is so much more clear because of you two and your encouraging and challenging feedback.

Thanks to all who have sought to be unifying voices in these polarizing times.

Finally, thanks to "The 7,000." This book exists in large part due to your faithful support. Whatever the Lord chooses to do with this, you share in the fruit of it.

Notes

Chapter 1: Roses Are Big

1. I want to be clear about something. I'm not attributing the fact that I
   was detained on the street as a possible suspect in a crime to "racism."
   It's perfectly logical to me that if a crime occurred in the vicinity where I
   happened to be walking that day and I also happened to fit the description of the suspect based on what was ascertained from eyewitnesses,
   then the officer on duty had an obligation to determine if I was, in fact,
   the perpetrator of the crime. That's just good police work. (The problem
   is that "fit the description" has been used as a pretext for illegal stops
   and searches of young Black and Brown men for who knows how long.)
   I won't even assume that Officer Shut Up, who was White, spoke to me
   that way because he's a "racist." He might have said the same exact thing
   if I was a White suspect. It's really only what the sergeant, who was also
   White, said to me—more than that, the way he said it—that caused me
   to file this under the "racism" section of my experiential rolodex.

Chapter 2:My New Life

1. The Cross Movement, "Cypha the Next Day," track 18 on *House of Representatives*, Cross Movement Records, 1999.
2. The Cross Movement, "Human Superstars," track 6 on *House of Representatives*, Cross Movement Records, 1999.
3. The Ambassador, "Psalm 23," track 12 on *Christology: In Layman's Terms*, Cross Movement Records, 2000.

Chapter 3: Lyrical Theology

1. Charles Wesley, "And Can It Be, That I Should Gain?" (1738), Public Domain, https://hymnary.org/text/and_can_it_be_that_i_should_gain.
2. Collin Hansen, *Young, Restless, Reformed: A Journalist's Journey with the New Calvinists* (Wheaton, IL: Crossway, 2008).
3. "Reformed Rap and Hip-Hop," *Christianity Today*, May 2011, https://www.christianitytoday.com/ct/2011/may/spot-reformedrap.html.
4. Propaganda, "Precious Puritans," track 7 on *Excellent*, Humble Beast, 2012.

Chapter 4: Voices from the Past

1. Committee on Mission to North America Pastoral Letter on Racism, PCA 32nd General Assembly, 2004.
2. Ibid.
3. Matthew J. Hall, "Historical Causes of the Stain of Racism in the Southern Baptist Convention," in *Removing the Stain of Racism from the Southern Baptist Convention*, Jarvis Williams and Kevin Jones, eds. (Nashville: B&H Academic, 2017), 9.
4. Albert Mohler, "Conceived in Sin, Called by the Gospel: The Root Cause of the Stain of Racism in the Southern Baptist Convention," in *Removing the Stain of Racism from the Southern Baptist Convention*, Williams and Kevin, eds., 3.
5. Jonathan Edwards, *The Works of Jonathan Edwards/Vol. 16: Letters and Personal Writings*, George S. Claghorn, ed. (New Haven, CT: Yale University, 1998), 801.
6. Ibid., 802–803.

7. Anthony Carter, *On Being Black and Reformed: A New Perspective on the African-American Christian Experience* (Phillipsburg, NJ: P&R Publishing, 2003), 134.

8. Marcus Ortega, "To the Reformed World: Minorities Are Here to Stay," April 1, 2016, https://reformedmargins.com/reformed-world-minorities-stay.

Chapter 5: Déjà Vu

1. Alan Yuhas, "Philadelphia's Osage Avenue Police Bombing, 30 Years On: 'This Story Is a Parable,'" *Guardian*, May 13, 2015, https://www.theguardian.com/us-news/2015/may/13/osage-avenue-bombing-philadelphia-30-years.

2. Chris Francescani, "George Zimmerman: Prelude to a Shooting," Reuters, April 25, 2012, https://www.reuters.com/article/us-usa-florida-shooting-zimmerman/george-zimmerman-prelude-to-a-shooting-idUSBRE83O18H20120425.

3. Sarah Pullman Bailey, "White Evangelicals Voted Overwhelmingly for Donald Trump, Exit Polls Show," *Washington Post*, November 9, 2016, https://www.washingtonpost.com/news/acts-of-faith/wp/2016/11/09/exit-polls-show-white-evangelicals-voted-overwhelmingly-for-donald-trump.

4. Campbell Robertson, "A Quiet Exodus: Why Black Worshipers Are Leaving White Evangelical Churches," *New York Times*, May 9, 2018, https://www.nytimes.com/2018/03/09/us/blacks-evangelical-churches.html.

5. Bob Bixby, "The Gospel in Black and White: A Missiological Perspective on Ferguson" was originally posted in 2014 online at redeemerfremont.com.

Chapter 6: Is Martin Luther My Homeboy?

1. Michael Reeves and Tim Chester, *Why the Reformation Still Matters* (Wheaton, IL: Crossway, 2016), 17.

2. Catechism of the Catholic Church. See also #97 and #100, http://www.vatican.va/archive/ENG0015/__PN.HTM.

3. Martin Luther, "The Diet of Worms: Luther's Final Answer," Henry Bettenson and Chris Maunder, *Documents of the Christian Church*, 4th ed. (Oxford: Oxford University Press, 2011), 214.

4. The Cambridge Declaration, Alliance of Confessing Evangelicals, April 20, 1996, https://www.alliancenet.org/cambridge-declaration.

5. Ibid.

6. Martin Luther, *Luther's Works*, vol. 34, Career of the Reformer IV (St. Louis: Concordia Publishing House, 1960), 336–37.

7. The Cambridge Declaration.

8. Ibid.

9. Ibid.

10. Shai Linne, "The Glory of God (Not to Us)," track 2 on *The Attributes of God*, Lamp Mode, 2011.

11. "Big God Theology" is a phrase that has been used in recent years as shorthand for God's sovereign rule over all things. It has particularly been used to describe the view of God adopted by many African Americans in the slavery era. See Thabiti Anyabwile's *The Decline of African American Theology* (Downers Grove, IL: IVP Academic, 2007), 65–73. Though he doesn't use the phrase in the book, the examples he cites have elsewhere been characterized as Big God Theology.

12. "The Low End Theory" is a double entendre. It's also the name of a popular hip-hop album from the early 1990s.

13. Contemporary theologians Michael Horton and Robert Godfrey have traced the "semper reformanda" slogan to a 1674 devotional work by the Dutch Reformed minister Jodocus van Lodenstein.

Chapter 7: Ethnicity and the Fall

1. J. Daniel Hays, *From Every People and Nation: A Biblical Theology of Race* (Downers Grove, IL: InterVarsity, 2003), 19.

2. See *The Faithful Preacher: Recapturing the Vision of Three Pioneering African-American Pastors* by Thabiti Anyabwile (Wheaton, IL: Crossway, 2007).

3. See *The Myth of Race: The Troubling Persistence of an Unscientific Idea* by Robert Wald Sussman (Cambridge, MA: Harvard University Press, 2016).

4. New Oxford American Dictionary (New York: Oxford University Press, 2005).

5. James Peoples and Garrick Bailey, *Humanity: An Introduction to Cultural Anthropology*, 9th ed. (Boston: Wadsworth Cengage Learning, 2010), 389.

6. "ethnos," 1484, HELPS Word Studies, Bible Hub, https://biblehub .com/greek/1484.htm.

7. Some people question the role ethnic hatred played in Jonah's anger over the repentance of the Ninevites. I personally believe that Jonah's resistance was due to the violence that the Assyrian military had inflicted on Israel and other nations for centuries at that point. But it wasn't just the military that repented. It was the whole city: men, women, young, old, "from the greatest to the least." Presumably, even people who hadn't participated in the violence. And yet Jonah was still angry. It's important to keep in mind the definition of ethnicity mentioned earlier: "people joined by practicing similar customs or common culture." His anger was toward God for showing mercy to a group of people (an ethnic group) that Jonah had come to despise.

8. Danielle Chemtob, "Wells Fargo to Pay Nearly $8 Million to Resolve Hiring Discrimination Accusations," August 25, 2020, *Charlotte Observer*, https://www.charlotteobserver.com/news/business/banking/ article245233685.html.

9. See *The New Jim Crow* by Michelle Alexander, (New York: The New Press, 2020).

10. Kirk Johnson, Richard Pérez-Peña, and John Eligon, "Rachel Dolezal, in Center of Storm, Is Defiant: 'I Identify as Black,'" *New York Times*, June 16, 2015, https://www.nytimes.com/2015/06/17/us/rachel-dolezal-nbc-today-show.html.

11. Edward Boyer, "Rescuers Describe Saving Beaten and Bloody Denny," *Los Angeles Times*, August 27, 1993, https://www.latimes.com/archives/ la-xpm-1993-08-27-mn-28517-story.html.

12. Frederick Douglass, *The Narrative of the Life of Frederick Douglass, an American Slave* (Boston: published at the Anti-Slavery Office, No. 25, Cornhill, 1849), 118.

Chapter 8: Father Abraham Had Many Sons

1. Petrus Antonius Laurentius Kantner (Pierre Kartner), "Vader Abraham," (Father Abraham).
2. Shai Linne, "God Made Me and You," track 3 on *Jesus Kids*, SDGFella Music, 2018.

Chapter 9: Ethnicity and Justification

1. "Question 33," *The Westminster Confession of Faith: Together with the Larger Catechism and the Shorter Catechism with the Scripture Proofs*, 3rd ed. (Atlanta: Committee for Christian Education and Publications, 1990), 12.
2. Ewald Plass, *What Luther Says: An Anthology*, vol. 2 (St. Louis: Concordia Publishing House, 1959), 702–704, 715.
3. "Question 81," *The Westminster Confession of Faith*, 25.
4. "Question 80," *The Westminster Confession of Faith*, 24.
5. See the book *The Great Exchange: My Sin for His Righteousness* by Jerry Bridges and Bob Bevington (Wheaton, IL: Crossway, 2007).
6. Timothy Keller, *The Meaning of Marriage: Facing the Complexities of Commitment with the Wisdom of God* (New York: Dutton, 2011), 48.

Chapter 11: Agree in the Lord

1. This recap tells how the stories played out over many months, and I referred to a variety of internet sources to gather the information.
2. See *Divided by Faith: Evangelical Religion and the Problem of Race in America* by Michael Emerson and Christian Smith (Cambridge, MA: Oxford University Press, 2000). Sympathy is necessary in order to bridge those gaps.
3. Excerpted from the Nicene Creed (transl. © 1988, Faith Alive Christian Resources/Christian Reformed Church in North America). All rights reserved worldwide. Used with permission.

Chapter 12: We Got Some Work to Do

1. Frederick Douglass, *The Narrative of the Life of Frederick Douglass, an American Slave* (Boston: published at the Anti-Slavery Office, No. 25, Cornhill, 1849), 118.
2. Harvie Conn, *Evangelism: Doing Justice and Preaching Grace* (Phillipsburg, NJ: P&R Publishing, 1982), 12.
3. *The Westminster Confession of Faith: Together with the Larger Catechism and the Shorter Catechism with the Scripture Proofs*, 3rd ed. (Atlanta: Committee for Christian Education and Publications, 1990), 2.1.
4. John Owen, *The Glory of Christ* (Chicago: Moody, 1949), 99.
5. "Stricken, Smitten and Afflicted," from the *Trinity Hymnal*, rev. ed. (Suwanee, GA: Great Commission Publications, 1990), 257.

Epilogue: Soon and Very Soon

1. See *Divided by Faith: Evangelical Religion and the Problem of Race in America* by Michael Emerson and Christian Smith (Cambridge, MA: Oxford University Press, 2000).
2. M. Night Shyamalan, *The Sixth Sense*, directed by M. Night Shyamalan (Burbank, CA: Buena Vista Pictures, 1999), film.
3. I first heard this articulated by Tim Keller. Shout out to TK.

As those who know the Creator, Christians should be leading the way in creativity.

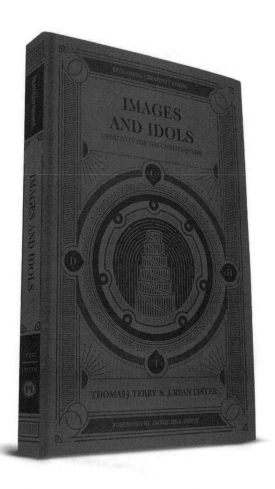